BENEDICT HUNT

DARK
PSYCHOLOGY
AND
MANIPULATION

HOW TO USE THE BEST TECHNIQUES OF PSYCHOLOGY AND MENTAL MANIPULATION TO YOUR ADVANTAGE!! DISCOVER SECRETS AND STRATEGIES TO INFLUENCE EVERYONE AND DEFEND YOURSELFS

© Copyright 2021 - Benedict Hunt

All rights reserved–

The content contained within this book may not be reproduced, duplicated or transmitted without direct written permission from the author or the publisher.

Under no circumstances will any blame or legal responsibility be held against the publisher, or author, for any damages, reparation, or monetary loss due to the information contained within this book. Either directly or indirectly.

Legal Notice

This book is copyright protected. This book is only for personal use. You cannot amend, distribute, sell, use, quote or paraphrase any part, or the content within this book, without the consent of the author or publisher.

Disclaimer Notice

Please note the information contained within this document is for educational and entertainment purposes only. All effort has been executed to present accurate, up to date, and reliable, complete information. No warranties of any kind are declared or implied. Readers acknowledge that the author is not engaging in the rendering of legal, financial, medical or professional advice. The content within this book has been derived from various sources. Please consult a licensed professional before attempting any techniques outlined in this book.

By reading this document, the reader agrees that under no circumstances is the author responsible for any losses, direct or indirect, which are incurred as a result of the use of information contained within this document, including, but not limited to, errors, omissions, or inaccuracies.

TABLE OF CONTENTS

INTRODUCTION

N ow, while all of us will try to manipulate another person on occasion to help us get things done or to get something we want, not everyone is easily manipulated. Sure, you could probably get someone to give you a ride on occasion, but that does not mean that you would be able to do some of the emotional and covert manipulative techniques that we talked about on them. There are some types of people who are more susceptible to being manipulated, who make the job of the manipulator easier, and these people will often find that they are not pulling the strings at all in their own lives.

So, how do you know if you are a prime target for a manipulator? Could you be one of those people who manipulators are looking for all the time? Some of the people who can be easily manipulated include:

Those who rely on others for information: If you rely on someone else for information, you are just asking for someone to try and fool you. You must be alert to the things that are going on around you, and you must learn to make informed decisions that use common sense. Otherwise, a manipulator will quickly take over, and you will just go along with them because it is the easiest path.

Those who do not think through their decisions: For those who like to think quickly, a manipulator is helpful to them. The manipulator can come in and help them make the decision. Someone who thinks through their decisions will not like the idea of someone else coming in and trying to do the work for them. But those who want to get the decision-making over with quickly will appreciate the help that the manipulator will give.

Those who have low self-confidence: Those who have low self-confidence are perfect targets. These individuals often are overlooked by others and may not have a lot of friends. The manipulator can come in and offer to be that friend and can work to build up the confidence of their target. As they are doing this, the target will feel indebted to the manipulator and will be more likely to do what the manipulator wants.

Those who respond to guilt: Guilt can be a powerful motivator, and a good manipulator will be able to use this to their advantage. These targets want to be helpful and do not want to feel guilty for not doing something that they should. A manipulator can play the victim card a little bit with this one, and they are sure to get this target to act the way that they want.

Those who like flattery: If you are someone who likes to listen to flattery and will chase it down, then you will be a very easy target for a manipulator. All the manipulator will need to do in this situation is start adding in some flattery. They could spend time with you, compliment you often and just be overall nice to you. These actions will stroke your ego, and you will open yourself up to do what the manipulator wants.

Those who are empathetic to others: This is a great option to go for as a manipulator. These people like to help others and are always falling for the next sob story they hear. They understand that people fall on hard times, and they want to be there to help. While their ideals may be altruistic, many people will take advantage of this. They simply need to make the target feel bad for them, such as telling them a sad story or letting them know that they, the manipulator, are used to this abuse. If they can do this properly, this kind of target will jump into helping them right away.

Those who become blinded by love: Manipulators love this kind of target because they will be able to make them fall deeply in love. They will say and do all the right things to make the target believe that they are in love. The target believes that they are so much in love that the other person would never harm them.

While it is possible for anyone to be manipulated during their lives, there are some people who are easier targets than others. If you fall into one of the categories above, it may be time to make some changes before someone tries to manipulate you and take over your life. Remember that the manipulator is not willing to work harder than they need to manipulate the other person. If they feel that someone will be at least a little bit difficult to manipulate, they will pick someone else to target.

YOU CAN'T CHANGE YOUR MANIPULATOR

It is impossible to change your manipulator and to try to do this is just going to result in heartache and more issues in your life. However, you can make changes in yourself that will make things more difficult for the manipulator and perhaps make them go away.

The moment that you stop pleasing, complying, or cooperating with the manipulator is the moment that they will leave you alone. The manipulator does not want to work hard for the control, and if you start putting up a fight, then they will take off and look for someone else.

There are many targets who believe that they can change their manipulator. They want to stay around in the hopes that the manipulator will suddenly realize what is going on and will want to make a change. However, this is never going to happen. While there may be a few manipulators who are unaware of the tactics that they are using, most manipulators are skilled at what they are doing, and they have been working for a long time to perfect their techniques. These individuals will be impossible to change. Even when they are confronted and made aware of how they are hurting the target, they will not find the motivation to change.

Most manipulators can disguise their motives by hiding behind a lot of layers of lies. It is impossible to add on all these layers without knowing exactly what you are doing, and it is unlikely that they care that you think it is a bad thing. If they can maintain control, they will be happy.

Since there are all these layers of lies that the manipulator must maintain, they will often use some tactics that are considered acceptable by society. This can just make it more confusing for the target. Some of the tactics that they may consider using include:

The manipulator will resort to caring for and loving their target for a time. They will spend some time showing the target how much they care for them. They use this love as a bargaining tool to get the target to do what they want.

The manipulator may try to overpower the target, sometimes making the target feel like the manipulator is the expert.

The manipulator can try to show the target how generous they are. They will show the target that they care because they are helping them out in any way they can. They may say that they are doing something to help the target, or they are doing it for the target's own good.

One thing that you should consider is that it is not a good idea to ask a manipulator what their true intentions and motives are. You are not going to get an honest answer at all. The manipulator is a skilled liar, and they will be able to keep it all hidden. Often, these questions will result in the manipulator getting defensive or angry towards you. Most manipulators have the idea that they deserve to do these things because they help them get to their goals, no matter what it takes.

THE FUNDAMENTALS OF DARK PSYCHOLOGY AND WHAT IT IS

D ark Psychology is the phenomenon by which individuals use strategies of inspiration, influence, control and intimidation to get what they need. Dark Psychology is the examination of the man circumstances to check how they get motivated and move after others and thus commits different criminal activities. All of humankind can potentially victimize other people. While many limits or suppress this inclination, some follow up on these impulses.

Those thoughts, emotions, insights and subjective dispensation systems are deliberated in Dark Psychology that leads to savage conduct that is contradictory to present identifications of human conduct. Dark Psychology says that 99.99% of the period there is a purpose behind criminal acts and harsh modes. Dark

Psychology hypothesizes there is an area inside the human mind that empowers a few people to submit dreadful acts without reason.

Dark Psychology says that all humanity can execute the pernicious plan towards others extending from being obtrusive and changeable states to untainted psychopathic behavior with no durable shrewdness. This is known as the Dark Continuum.

All humans are made with some of the darker sides inside them. No one can claim that he or she is pure of any evil side. Some people think of this side as criminal, immoral and pathological. The fact is some tend to show their darker side while some do not have that caliber.

Dark Psychology presents a third philosophical development that sees these practices not quite the same as religious dogmas and contemporary sociology hypotheses.

Dark Psychology suggests that some individuals commit these acts, and they do not do because of power, cash, sex, or some other known reason. They commit these awful acts without an objective. Some people damage and harm others for satisfying themselves. Dark psychology tends to reside in itself where someone hurts others without any clarification, objective and cause.

Dark Psychology claims that we all have an innate ability to copy the behaviors of others. This ability precedes our emotions, thoughts and perceptions. We have our emotions and feelings so we act rudely in one or another. We all have the innate thinking of hurting others without any cause and being unkind to others.

In reality, we perceive ourselves as kind and humble creatures. We all have such emotions and thoughts but sometimes we are not ready to accept them. Dark Psychology presents some individuals who have these similar ideas, emotions and perceptions, and they don't hesitate and pursue their plans. The main difference is some action on their projects, but others have those feelings for a short interval of time, and they disappear after that, leaving no intent of doing such a thing. The part that triggers our predatory behavior is analyzed in the phenomenon of Dark Psychology. Lack of apparent rational impulse, wholeness, loss of predictability and perception are remarkable characteristics of the behavioral. Dark Psychology understands this given human condition is modified or expansion of evolution. First, we need to think that we evolved from some animals and we are the best of all animals. Now assume that being the best beings does not make us detached from our animal senses and predatory nature.

Considering it right if you contribute to evolution, then you think that all manners and behaviors relate to three primary instincts. Sex, aggression and intelligence are the three fundamental human drives. Survival of the fittest and changing of the characters are key principles of evolution.

The thing that makes us best among all is our control over our thinking and perceptions. Universally, males fight till their death with immense power. This is the ritual of human societies. All actions, violence and brutality explain a certain evolution.

We tend to see that when animals hunt, they often chase and kill the weakest of the crowd. The purpose of this action is to lessen the probability of their death. The animal world behaves in that manner. In this study of dark psychology, we will learn about its application to the species present on earth. The great writers have tried their best to discuss this phenomenon. There are only humans that can cause harm to others without any cause or purpose. Dark Psychology believes there is a part of the human, which feeds vicious and wicked behaviors.

According to Dark Psychology, the dark side of humans is unpredictable. Some people torture, rape, murder and violate without any cause or purpose. Dark Psychology talks to these activities of a man as a predator hunting prey without any reason. We humans are strangely dangerous to ourselves and even to other living creatures.

The more the reader can figure Dark Psychology, the better set up they become to decrease their odds of exploitation by human predators. Before continuing, it is important to have an awareness of Dark Psychology.

SIX PRINCIPLES TO UNDERSTANDING DARK PSYCHOLOGY

The following are six principles essential to understanding Dark Psychology:

1. Dark Psychology is a general part of the human condition and has had its impact from the beginning. All societies, social orders and the individuals who live in

them keep up this aspect of human health. The most kindhearted individuals known have this field of evil; however, they never followed it and have lower frequencies of rough ideas and emotions.

2. Dark Psychology is the examination of the human condition as it correlates with people groups' thoughts, emotions and perceptions identified with this natural potential to hurt others without any cause. Given that all manner is purposive and goal-oriented, Dark Psychology suggests that the less the person stays in the "dark hole" of evilness, the fewer chances there are for their purpose of inspiration.

3. There are a lot of historical instances where we can see unusual and dangerous activities. Currently, we can characterize a psychopath as a predator without regrets. Dark Psychology says that there is a continuum of seriousness extending from ideas and emotions of destruction to extreme exploitation without reason.

4. Dark psychology is considered as a wide scope of brutality. An honest description would analyze Ted Bundy and Jeffrey Dahmer. Both were extreme mental cases and horrifying in their activities. The thing that matters is Dahmer committed his murders for his odd requirement for friendship while Ted Bundy killed out of pure psychopathic evilness. Both are higher on the Dark Continuum, yet one, Jeffrey Dahmer, can be better comprehended as he wanted to be loved.

5. Dark Psychology presumes all individuals have a potential for cruelty. This potential is inborn in all people, and different inner and outside components increase

the likelihood of this possibility to show uncertainly. These practices are ruthless and occur occasionally. Dark Psychology is exclusively a human phenomenon and shared by no other living being. Violence and brutality may exist in other living beings, yet humans are the main kinds that can do without reason.

6. A comprehension of the unknown triggers of Dark Psychology would better empower society to perceive, analyze and reduce the danger in its impact. Learning the ideas of Dark Psychology talks about its advantages as well. Besides, knowing the fundamentals of Dark Psychology accommodates our unique developmental reason for attempting to stay.

We were likely to teach others by expanding their awareness, making a change in their existence to improve things and inspiring them to instruct others to try to figure out how to reduce the possibility of being the victim of these evil forces and how dark psychology helps with this.

We all have our dark sides being a part of the human condition, yet not known lately. As this author has recently mentioned, Dark Psychology incorporates all types of brutal and violent behaviors.

This writer tries to look at Dark Psychology's starting point and nature to see how the healthy, intelligent individual can end up in the news, having an outrage behavior nobody could have expected. It is astonishing how people with good mental health might take an interest in, or permit such violence.

Great outrages are clear from history. There are enormous examples including the destruction that happened during World War II. As represented above, Dark Psychology is actual and alive, which requires a genuine discussion. As you keep on investigating the principles and fundamentals of Dark Psychology, a psychological structure of understanding will gradually create.

DARK CONTINUUM

The Dark Continuum is a significant component to understand the dark sector of humanity. The Dark Continuum is a hypothetical logical line or concentric circles that all corrupt criminals and sadist behavior lie. The Dark Continuum incorporates thoughts, emotions, observations and activities experienced or potentially dedicated by people. The continuum ranges from purposeful to purposeless.

Mental appearances of Dark Psychology lie to one side of the continuum and they are as harmful as physical acts. The Dark Continuum isn't a scale of seriousness but ranges from poor to more terrible. When this author further grows his theory of the Dark Continuum, you will have a reasonable represented line describing all types of Dark Psychology running from purposeful to purposeless.

DARK FACTOR

The Dark Factor is characterized as the part that is there in our personality as a core part of the human condition. This idea is so conceptual that it is difficult to understand in words. As per an online dictionary, a factor is whatever contributes causally to an outcome, i.e., various elements determined the result. This author will try to extrapolate for you in a consistent tone how Dark Factor takes after a condition.

The Dark Factor is an exact condition, however, a hypothetical one. The Dark Factor is something a person encounters, which builds the possibility of engaging in violent conduct.

Even though exploration has proposed that youngsters who experience childhood in an abusive family become abusers themselves, this doesn't mean every mishandled kid develops to become violent. It is just a single aspect of a large number of experiences and conditions that add to the Dark Factor.

The quantity of components that are associated with the Dark Factor condition is enormous. It isn't the number of parts making Dark Factor outrageous. It is the effect that encounters an individual's emotional processing that makes the Dark Factor dangerous. A portion of these aspects incorporates hereditary qualities, relational characteristics, psychological insight, peer acceptance, sensitive treatment, developmental accomplishments and experiences.

THE DARK TRIAD

There are many ways to describe the cruel and inconsiderate among us. We can say they are mean, callous, awful, immoral, rude, depraved, unfeeling, heartless and shady. We can talk endlessly about the qualities of the worst among us, but in the science of psychology, three qualities have emerged that best describe these sorts of people. We call these qualities "The Dark Triad." The dark triad consists of narcissism, psychopathy and Machiavellianism.

The dark triad is known to be the base of a lot of bad behavior, including lying, cheating, manipulation, impulsivity, even murder and rape. It can be thought of as both a set of personality traits that can exist at varying levels in different individuals and also a device used by those high in these qualities to try to get away with mistreating others in all sorts of ways to satisfy themselves and get what they want easily and quickly.

The operative word here is quick—while those whose personalities strongly exhibit personality components of the dark triad may get what they want oftentimes, their relationships are strained, destructive and fleeting. Naturally, those around them often catch on to their ways and, like a parasite, they need to find a new person or people to victimize. Now that we have some basic information, we can go into more depth about the three components—narcissism, psychopathy and Machiavellianism.

NARCISSISM

At its most basic, narcissism describes a sense of extreme entitlement, lack of empathy and excessive admiration of oneself. The word comes from the Greek myth of Narcissus, a young man who was so beautiful that he fell in love with his own reflection. He was callous and condescending towards those who loved him and drove some to commit suicide to prove their undying admiration for him. There are many signs an individual is narcissistic, and you have most likely met someone who displays this personality trait.

One of the most obvious signs of a narcissist is an excessive preoccupation with how they are perceived by others. They may spend an excessive amount of time grooming themselves and constantly presenting themselves in a light so positive that it treads on dishonesty. The narcissist wants to be seen as a fabulous human being, constantly living it up and showing off their success and importance. They may exaggerate their achievements, social climb, or name drop about which important people they rub shoulders with.

In addition, a narcissist is an arrogant person who believes themselves to be more capable, important and worthy than those around them. They are often exploitative and lacking in empathy, which means that they will use others to get what they want, with no mind that it may be hurtful to the victim. Narcissists are able to do this because they view others as extensions of themselves and are unable to fathom that others have priorities that are dissimilar to their own—no favor is too big to ask for, and the narcissist's self-centeredness makes them believe that they are justified in their actions. The narcissist believes their needs are above those of others—why shouldn't others be extra considerate of them.

Think you've seen anger? Just wait until you meet narcissistic rage. Narcissistic rage is the outcome of a narcissistic injury. A narcissistic injury afflicts a narcissistic person when their grandiose opinion of themselves is challenged or shown to be faulty. For example, a narcissistic injury can come from being rejected by a potential romantic partner or getting turned down from a job. Having a response to rejection and disappointment this easily triggered is the result of childhood trauma, such as a neglectful or abusive parent. The child, who senses that their parent does not love them, develops a grandiose persona in order to hide their deep feelings of inadequacy and shame and to convince themselves that they will be invulnerable to such suffering at the hands of another ever again. Essentially, a narcissist is constantly trying to cover up how insecure they really feel by pretending they are the greatest, most fabulous and accomplished human being of all time.

Once the injury occurs, the narcissist may fly into what is known as narcissistic rage. They will be unable to regulate their emotions and actions. The actions resulting from narcissistic rage can range anywhere from silent treatment and temporarily withdrawing from others all the way to physical violence and serious abuse. Narcissistic rage occurs because the narcissistic injury is simply too much to bear. To the narcissist, it calls into question how great they actually are and exposes them as imperfect beings.

There are many telltale signs of a narcissist and knowing some of their common behaviors can make them easier to spot. For one thing, they will take credit for good things that happen to them and blame bad outcomes on others, no matter what the reality of the situation is. If they get a bad grade on a project, they will insist that the professor has it out for them or that the grading process was unfair. If they have a good outcome, say someone of their preferred sex being friendly, they may insist this person was flirting with them. The narcissist wants to bend every story to present themselves in the most positive light and will not entertain any possibility that they may be wrong about something.

A narcissistic person is also obsessed with perfection. Not only do they hold themselves to high standards, which they often believe themselves to meet, but they also hold entities external to themselves to such a standard. The narcissist expects the people around them to behave perfectly, for events they attend to be perfect and their circumstances to be perfect. They will become irate if they feel others have not met their expectations, even if they are unreasonable.

Another sign you may be dealing with a narcissist is that they speak in extremes about those around them. For example, they may profess how "special" you are and how much they love you one day, but as soon as you irritate them, they will disparage, insult, or neglect you. Despite a close relationship, a narcissist will always seem fairly uninterested in you as a person. You may tell them you had a bad day, or an interesting story about your day, and they will respond by talking about themselves. We have all had conversations like this—it's almost jarring. There you are, drinking coffee with a friend and believing both your and your friend's needs hold equal weight in the conversation when they suggest otherwise by talking about themselves nonstop. They will ask you a few questions about yourself and if they do, they seem to lose interest once you begin to reply. In short, what's the biggest sign someone is a narcissist? A narcissist will make you wonder if their life motto is "It's all about me!"

PSYCHOPATHY

We often picture a psychopathic person to be a serial killer or a career criminal. In fiction, Patrick Bateman of American Psycho is seen as the quintessential psychopath—charming, brilliant and unfathomably evil. Most psychopaths though will seem pretty normal to us. They are our co-workers sometimes, have been our classmates and maybe even our lovers and friends.

Psychopathy is referred to as Antisocial Personality Disorder (ASPD) in clinical settings. Psychopathy can exist along a spectrum; it is not an all-or-nothing quality. If someone were to take a personality test, they may score significantly higher than the population average on psychopathic tendencies but may still fall short of the necessary criteria for an ASPD diagnosis or may not exhibit antisocial behaviors sufficient for a diagnosis.

So, what characterizes psychopathy? First of all, psychopaths seem normal. They can be perfectly pleasant in conversations and give no hint about who they truly are. Underneath the normal exterior though, a psychopath is wicked. The psychopath lacks conscience, empathy and remorse. Because these qualities are absent, they are manipulative, self-serving and exploitative. Some even become criminals.

Another quality that defines psychopaths is a very high sensitivity to reward—when they want something, they want it badly, and they will do whatever is necessary to satisfy themselves. Many psychopaths are promiscuous and have many one-night stands. Being extra sensitive to reward combined with callousness and insensitivity means that psychopaths do not care about who gets hurt when they seek whatever appeals to them at the moment. Speaking of rewards, psychopaths will frequently use others to get what they want. They are keen on developing intimacy and trust, but once the main goal has been achieved, the psychopath discards the person they used, some-times leaving a trail of emotional or financial devasta-tion. Most psychopaths do not get treatment for ASPD. Not only do they believe there is nothing wrong with them, but their traits seem fairly fixed. Therapy and medication do not help change their thought patterns or often sadistic methods of controlling others. Con-sider yourself lucky if you have not been affected by a psychopath. They often wreak havoc on the lives of those they get close to.

In general, psychopaths will often seem to lack emotion. If a tragedy occurs, they may seem impossibly unaffected. They are also practically fearless com-pared to the rest of us—they are afraid of neither get-ting hurt nor getting caught. Overall, their emotions are shallow. They may enjoy someone's company, but they don't really care about this person. The psychopath of-ten lives for pleasure and power—human connection and emotion mean little to them.

Like narcissists, psychopaths also have a hard time accepting responsibility. Because of this and their lack of fear, they are often reckless and irresponsible. Not only do they behave irresponsibly, but they also insist that whatever they have caused is not their fault. Eventually, even if a psychopath is forced to accept blame, they will seem not to care. They do not see their irresponsible ways as an indictment of their skills, character, or ability. They see no reason to change be-cause it's always someone else's fault.

Last but not least in the most important traits to look out for are the psychopath's intense selfishness and egocentricity. The psychopath often lives a para-sitic lifestyle, which is to say they use others to meet their own needs without a thought about how this may affect the victim being bled dry. What does this look like? A psychopath may get close to you and then con-stantly ask you for money, whether or not they have enough of their own. If you are married to a psycho-path, you are probably the one who constantly cleans the house and cooks dinner unless your psychopathic spouse sees an incentive to complete those tasks. Of-ten, this is how psychopaths destroy lives. They may have children with a partner who feeds and cares for them and abandon this family eventually. They often take and take and take until their partner is completely broke and financially destitute. This is the parasitic life-style at play—the psychopath will suck your blood without you even noticing until you have none left. Once there is nothing for the parasite to take, they cut and run because you have nothing left to give them. It is estimated that up to twenty-five percent of incarcer-ated individuals suffer from ASPD.

MACHIAVELLIANISM

Before we get into Machiavellianism, let us un-derstand the word's namesake, Niccolò Machiavelli. Niccolò Machiavelli was an Italian statesman during the Italian Renaissance in the fifteenth and sixteenth centuries. He was a diplomat, politician, secretary, phi-losopher, poet, historian, humanist and playwright. He is known today for his book "Il Principe" or "The Prince." The book is a deep analysis into the acquisition and maintenance of political power, written so Machiavelli could return to Italian politics from exile and hopefully be appointed a political advisory position by the Medici family. The book was so shocking at the time that Machiavelli was labeled an atheist. Machiavelli advocated for ruthless, cunning and strategic methods of gaining and keeping political power. He is often credited with the saying, "the ends justify the means."

Given this introduction of Machiavelli the man, a deeper discussion of Machiavellianism as a member of the dark triad is appropriate. Machiavellianism includes low empathy, prioritizing power over others, strong ambition and exploitation of others for personal gain. Machiavellianism is different from psychopathy because of the Machiavellian's emphasis on exploitation for personal gain, whereas a psychopath's very nature is insensitivity and callousness no matter what.

The Machiavellian believes human nature is inherently evil and that deception is a justifiable way to attain goals and success. They generally undervalue human connection and overvalue wealth and power. They believe depending on others and cultivating meaningful emotional relationships is a worthless endeavor. When they manipulate or exploit others, they believe they have acted with reason and can justify their actions. They will do something terrible to complete a goal and when confronted, they will say, "Hey, I got the job done, right? It all worked out."

So, how do you know you're dealing with a Machiavellian? The Machiavellian is notoriously low on empathy; human connection always comes second to achievement and personal gain. To a Machiavellian, people are often conduits to other things—money, power, sex, or whatever else may seem worthwhile to achieve. Machiavellians are known to lie and exploit, when necessary, in order to get what they want.

Another common quality of Machiavellians is their penchant for strategy and calculation. A Machiavellian is good at sizing up others. They can read the room so to speak and are perceptive of others' thoughts, feelings and weaknesses, despite the low empathy that accompanies Machiavellianism. Due to this calculating nature, these people tend to be patient. They are constantly collecting information and analyzing it to use to their best advantage. They know how to plan and wait for their rewards.

The demeanor of a Machiavellian often falls into one of two camps. They either seem aloof and emotionally distant or charming and friendly. Note that both of these demeanors may be present in the same person; someone may be charming and friendly, but reveal so little about themselves that you may become suspicious or realize well into a relationship of any kind with the Machiavellian that you know little about them. This is deliberate, as the Machiavellian generally prefers not to share their true intentions with others.

With respect to their morals, Machiavellians are unlike psychopaths. While the psychopath simply lacks morals, the Machiavellian is scattered, inconsistent and ill-defined. The Machiavellian may claim to have certain ethical principles they value highly, but they are certainly willing to ignore them if they can justify doing so. Generally speaking, they have little respect for humanity as a whole. They think it is inherently evil, or at the very least not good, and are usually cynical.

DARK PSYCHOLOGY: 10 WAYS TO MANIPULATE PEOPLE

Manipulation is a social influence that aims to change the behavior or perception of others through indirect, deceptive, or vile strategies. For example, people such as friends, family and doctors can persuade them to change unhelpful habits and behaviors.

GASLIGHTING

"Puffing up is a manipulative strategy that can be described in three different variations of words: "That didn't happen," "You can't imagine," and "Are you crazy?" Gaslighting may be one of the most insidious manipulative strategies at the moment because it will distort and erode your sense of reality. It will weaken your ability to trust yourself, and inevitably make you lose grounds to justify abuse.

How can you fight back? Placing yourself in real-ity—sometimes writing down when things happen, telling friends, or reiterating your experience with support net-works can help counteract this exciting effect.

PROJECTION

Do you know when poisonous people claim that all the filth surrounding them is not their fault, but yours? That is pro-jection. We have all done some, but narcissists and psychopaths have done a lot. Projection is a defense mechanism used to re-place others' negative behaviors and traits by attributing them to others. Solution? Don't project your sympathy or compassion on poisonous people, and don't have any poisonous person's predic-tions. Projecting our conscience and value system onto others may lead to further exploitation.

GENERAL

You said that colleagues sometimes fail to con-sider the long-term impact of individual financial deci-sions. The office psychopath claimed that you called him "a loose cannon." You pointed out that if X, Y and Z conditions occur, the transaction may go south. Your narcissistic colleague told your boss that you said the deal was a "disaster." How is this going? Not just be-cause your nemesis doesn't understand what you are talking about. It is that he or she is not interested in understanding.

Vicious narcissists are not always ideological planners—many of them are ideologically lazy. Instead of spending time carefully considering different points of view, they summarize everything you say and publish. It is a general statement and does not recognize your nuances. Arguing or considering the multiple points of view you pay tribute to. To solve this problem, please stick to your truths and resist general statements by realizing that they are black and white illogical forms of thinking.

MOVE THE TARGET ROD

Abusive narcissists and social perverts use a logical fallacy, that is, "move the target column" to ensure that they have an excellent reason always to dissatisfy you. It is even if you had provided all the evidence in the world for verification. When your argument or action was taken to satisfy their request, they put forward another expectation of you or asked for more evidence.

Don't play that game. "Verify and approve of yourself. Knowing that you are enough does not have to make yourself feel persistently insufficient or unworthy to some extent," Alabi suggested.

CHANGE THE THEME

Switching the conversation topic sounds innocent, but in the master Manipulator's hands, changing the subject becomes a means of avoiding accountability. The anesthetist does not want you to be a topic that makes them responsible for anything, so they will re-schedule the discussion to benefit them.

If you allow, this kind of thing may go on forever, preventing you from actually participating in the issue. Try to fight back with the "broken record method": Continue to state the facts and don't distract them. Redirect them by saying, "This is not what I'm talking about. Let's continue to focus on the real problem." If they're not interested, please get out of it and focus on more constructive things.

GIVING OUT TITLES

Because you have been dealing with this problem since you encountered the first playground overlord, it doesn't make it more destructive (and continues until the presidential political period). It cannot be tolerated at all. The important thing is to end any interactions that include names and communicate interactions that you won't tolerate. Don't internalize: realize that they resort to names because they lack advanced methods.

SMEAR MOVEMENT

When toxic substances can't control what you think of yourself, they will start to control how others think about you; when you are marked as toxic, they will play hard. Sometimes the real evil genius will even split and conquer, pitting two people or groups against each other. Don't let them succeed. Record any form of harassment and make sure not to raise the bait and let this person's terrorist behavior trigger your behavior in a negative way that is falsely attributable to you.

DEVALUATION

Be careful when a colleague seems to love you while violently denying the last person in your position. Narcissistic abusers always do this. They devalue their sexual behavior to their new partner. Eventually, the new partner begins to suffer the same abuse as the narcissist's former partner. But this dynamic may happen in a professional domain and personal domain. A simple understanding of this phenomenon is the first step to deal with it. Be aware that how a person treats or talks about others may translate into the way they treat you in the future.

MISCHIEF

The problem is not your sense of humor, but the hidden intention of the joke. Covert narcissists like to make malicious comments at their own expense. These comments are usually dressed up as "joking" to say shocking things while still maintaining innocence and calm behavior. However, anytime you feel insensitive to insensitive behavior, an angry, stern word, you are accused of having no sense of humor. Don't let the office abuser make you think this is all innocent fun—it is not.

TRIANGULATION

One of the smartest ways for a truly toxic person to distract you is to focus your attention on others' so-called threats. It is called triangulation. Narcissists like to "repay" what others say about you. To resist this strategy, please be aware that the third party in the drama is also manipulated. She is another victim, not your enemy.

12 MANIPULATION TECHNIQUES YOUR COLLEAGUES USE TO HURT YOU

You would dance like a happy colleague singing in an ideal world and even the bad guys would be kind and famous for their ominous makeup and creepy costumes. Unfortunately, this is not the case in the real world. You may be the same happy employee in a Disney movie, surrounded by singing birds and chi flowers, but the bad guy will not wear ridiculous costumes, surrounded by a group of lads!

Among your pleased friends, there may be some people who will praise you, seem to support you, or even laugh at your jokes, while secretly digging a big hole for you. These bad guys are so dangerous because they can handle any situation, make you look bad and shine like a cutting-edge meat cleaver. These manipulators have nothing to lose; they can control your feelings with all their strength. Stay with them long enough and you will find yourself feeling like a worthless bastard.

BUILD CONFIDENCE

You are like the smartest person I have ever met. Narcissistic manipulators need to get the attention of everyone around them. So, when you join someone for the first time and find that you immediately attract your new friends, beware! Such people usually give you all the compliments in the book at the beginning to attract you. After finishing, they can play you like Ronaldo. Although it's so sensational and likable, it's best to stay rooted. A few tempting words may be the perfect trap for the Manipulator to lure you into completing the humble report he has been delaying. And don't think that you will get good evaluations for it. It will be all the pain; there is always no gain, you sweet naive!

CHANGE YOUR REALITY

I believe you are just imagining. How often do you get some negative things from a friend/colleague/relative? What did you do and point out these mistakes just to laugh at them? A typical narcissist/manipulator/psychological communicator relies on changing reality so that you not only think that what you say has never happened, but that you are losing this state. After long enough, you will gradually start to doubt everything and become your crazy fantasy.

HIGHLIGHT DEFECTS

Have you ever asked yourself why I did not perform well? The narcissistic Manipulator is technically called a projection, which ensures that his shortcomings are nothing but your weaknesses. In a sense, this strategy is particularly useful when the narcissist needs to explain his bad behavior by shifting responsibility to the variable shoulders. You may hear cheating spouses say: I am not cheating. Arrogance is your delusion and persistence. Or the head of government might say that if people are not willing to stop questioning me, I can make this country run better. Unlike physical abuse, the transferor projection of blame can cause moral and emotional damage to the victim and cause disability. These roles may conceal their inefficiency or lack of productivity at work and find a way to blame it on you. If you give me a better project to deal with, I will do better. You are not a good manager.

IRRELEVANT DIGRESSIONS WIN CONTROVERSY

So, you don't like big beards? You must like Hitler! For manipulating narcissists, a very well-known strategy is to lead arguments or conversations to a completely different dimension, mainly voting on justice or sensitive things. The idea is to upset or frustrate you by taking some form of a prominent point that is entirely unrelated to the last discussion. It comes from a very unsafe place in their hearts. The divergent thoughts turned into a threat to their arrogance. Traditionally, politicians often use this manipulation strategy to make the masses oppose any form of rational opposition. If you disagree with the current policy, you must not love your country!

TRUST YOUR WORDS

Your opinion is irrelevant. You are too emotional. To please your opinion, narcissists are likely to put some wrong labels on you to help them eliminate contemplation and fights. With the demand for social media, we now see online bullies emerging from wood products and making high-profile general comments on targets. Most of these statements have no reasonable basis and no other opinions. They are only used to minimize and degrade the target point. The trend is to move away from logic and cloud everything.

EXTREME LABELS

You not only think that I am wrong. You believe I will never be right. Narcissists often make absurd extreme statements to show everyone how biased you are. Motivation? Simply emphasize your unfairness. Suppose a colleague is joking about the way you dress.

You just need to point it out to him. If he proceeds to be a narcissist, he will surely be famous for fighting back. Are you that sensitive?

NEVER APPRECIATE

So, do you think you can dance? Can you do math while dancing? You are not satisfied with the narcissistic Manipulator. Because if you do, then you are no longer their punching bag. Without you to feed their massive self-expansion, they will have to go through the tedious process of finding another minion. It is your typical narcissistic time!

> ➢ Is it still single?
> ➢ Oh! When did you get married?
> ➢ So long? And do you still have no children?
> ➢ Do you? Are you a teenager now?

Are you worried that they will become young people and soon get married and settle with their children?

CRUEL JOKES AND PAINFUL IRONY

Did you stay up late to do this analysis? I hope you have told me; otherwise, I won't take 15 minutes to finish it this morning. Toxic people like to disappoint victims by making jokes or taunts without knowing it. Mainly done in other people's presence, the purpose is to make you look smarter while looking like Daffy Duck. Although not necessarily only for toxic people, it becomes a feature among narcissists when they shoot regardless of the receiver's feelings.

BELITTLE YOUR ACHIEVEMENTS

It is a great plan, and everyone is talking about it. Are you sure this is what you require to show your boss? Narcissists can act very gently, taking all the time they want first to make you believe that they value everything in their lives. Once achieved, they will begin gradually alienating you from everything you like to control you fully. They will use false third-party claims to make others accomplices in their Machiavellian plan to destroy you.

At work, you may find colleagues/bosses who no longer appreciates your talents and contributions for some time, thus making you doubt everything you used to be good at. A toxic boss may lead you to believe that you may be better than some prior workers and slowly deal with your abuse.

BAIT, THEN PLAY THE VICTIM

I don't know why he shouted. I just asked him about his monthly report. Toxic people may play thinking games that are too complicated for the normal brain. They will provoke their targets with sensational jabs and comments and then use their natural confrontational responses to prove that their targets are unreasonable. They like to lure their goals into situations that indicate that they are victims of abuse. In workplaces where impressions matter, your visible aggression will be negatively evaluated. No one wants to care about the events that led to this outbreak.

BREAK THE LIMIT

Sorry, I called you fool the other day. But when you give a speech like a fool, what can I say! If you think you have overcome the Manipulator's attempt to devalue yourself, beware of more massive attempts. Robots like to be able to break through the limit to test the final breakthrough point.

SECRET AND PUBLIC THREATS TO EXERCISE CONTROL

How dare you send the report directly to the boss? Didn't I tell you to let me verify everything? It is the last choice of the Manipulator. They are usually brilliant in disguising their way. However, if you happen to be someone who is not bothered by other things at all, they will feel that their control is threatened. Then they turned to more local responses, such as threats and calls.

EVERYTHING ABOUT THE MANIPULATORS, THEIR BEHAVIOR AND CHARACTERISTICS

Manipulation is something that we have all dealt with, but it is not as easy to identify as it seems. Yes, sometimes, even though people are manipulating you, it won't harm you in any way. But on several occasions, manipulation can have severe consequences because the manipulator might have some selfish motives.

Think about it—did you ever feel someone is trying to control you or pressurize you into doing something that you don't want to do? It can be with someone you are involved in a close relationship with or even a run-in with some acquaintance of yours. Manipulation can be of different types—it can be your emotionally abusive partner, or it can also be a salesperson who is incessantly trying to sell you something that you don't want to buy. Therapists define manipulation as a strategy that is primarily an unhealthy psychological practice and it is implemented by those people who want to get things their way and yet don't have it in them to ask for it directly. The tactics used by a manipulator are abusive and deceptive. But in some cases, you might not recognize manipulation right away because the manipulator acts in a friendly way in order to put their ulterior motive under a veil. In these cases, the victim is not able to realize that someone is manipulating them.

It becomes harder to spot a manipulator even more for those who have grown up in households where manipulation was a usual thing. Even though you might feel angry from time to time, but the manipulator will use feelings like sympathy and try to reason with you on the surface, and so, gradually, your instincts are overridden by this fake pleasantness of the manipulator. Manipulation tactics are very often used by codependent people mainly because they do not know how they can be assertive or direct about their feelings. So, in order to get what they want, they use manipulation. On the other hand, codependent people are also very easy prey for other manipulators, especially narcissists.

Here, I am going to explain some traits to you that will help you identify a manipulator.

THEY ALWAYS USE THE VICTIM CARD

Most expert manipulators will make you feel guilty about one thing or the other. They take the help of constant victimization. In fact, they probably bring up a difficult phase of their life from time to time and play the "trauma wild card" in front of you whenever they feel that they can't get things their way. After that, they also try to use that traumatic experience to justify anything bad that they have done. It can be anything like the death of a family member, traumatic childhood, abusive ex-partner and so on. There is a certain level of inflated pride in the way they display their emotional scars, and you will automatically feel the vibe. They simply love to brag about whatever wrong that has happened in their life.

When someone poses to be the victim in all situations, they do experience some advantages over others, the major one being no one is going to criticize them. Moreover, everyone tries to understand their situation, empathize with them and treat them with compassion. The moment someone questions them, that person would be declared insensitive. So, they can hide behind their trauma, and people will automatically accept that whatever they are saying is true. But it has been often noticed that when someone is playing this victim card over and over again, they are actually hiding blackmail. I will not disagree with you that sometimes, there are cases where people are truly victims of some situations, but that doesn't mean that their state of being a victim is going to last forever.

So, how can you identify whether someone is really a victim or just a victim manipulator? Well, here are some of the things that you should look out for:

The manipulators will not ask for anything directly, but they do have wants that they want to satisfy. So, they say something that is regretful or in the form of a complaint. For example: "Nobody understands my pain and the hurdles I have crossed." When someone says this, it's easy for a person to get confused about whether the victim is trying to ask you for help, or are they simply angry at the fact that it was not as difficult for you as it was for them. If someone is trying to be manipulative, then you will experience a feeling of guilt every time you are with them. No matter what conversation you are having, they will make you feel that you have a role to play in their misery and so you should be guilty of it. All of this sadness emanating from the manipulator will put you in discomfort.

When someone is a victim manipulator, they will often keep reminding you of the evil motives in every people around you. But when it comes to their own misdeeds, they will use the "trauma card" to justify their actions. If you go on to criticize them as a hypocrite, they will call you callous and insensitive. And no one wants to hear these things, so victim manipulators use this as their weapon.

These manipulators also have the habit of making sacrifices even when no one asked them to. After that, they will keep boasting about everything they did for you.

THEY USE SUBTLE THREATS

Emotional blackmail or subtle threats is another thing that will help you spot the manipulators. It can be in the form of various things like shame, intimidation, or even rage. The threats they will make might not always be directly hurled at you. Sometimes they are subtle and indirect, but nonetheless, they are threats, and it is, in fact, a very commonly used tactic. Be it domestic abuse or huge political leaders; every manipulator has used threats at some point or the other. The main thing about this tactic is that the manipulator will openly tell you about the worst outcome that can happen and then pose it to you as a threat. For example, "If you don't curb your eating, no one is going to date you because, in a few months, you will look like an elephant." So, even if you give them any scientific information, they are simply not going to hear from you. This kind of behavior might be a result of several things. For example, if someone is not happy because you are eating pizza and they cannot because they are on a strict diet, they might manipulate you into not eating pizza as well. But the problem is, these people don't know how to say things directly, and so they hide behind toxic manipulation. They think that if they imply that a catastrophe will happen if you don't listen to them, then you will do as they say.

THEY QUESTION YOUR SANITY

Another very notable characteristic of manipulators is that whenever you are in an argument with them, they will say something or do something that will make you question your sanity. In other terms, they use gaslighting. For example, if you narrate an incident to them, do they believe at one go, or do they question you regarding whether all the facts were correct? Do they believe your side of the story, or do they change the narration and make it seem that everything was your fault? If you are going for the latter part of each of these questions, then it is clear that you are dealing with a manipulator who uses gaslighting tactics to get what they want.

A manipulator is using tactics of emotional abuse if he/she is trying to gaslight you. There are so many adverse effects of gaslighting on the mental health of the victim because it leads to severe anxiety and can even lead to panic attacks and nervous breakdowns in the future. Here is a list of things that happen if you are with a manipulative person who is trying to use gaslighting to gain the upper hand:

Whenever you have a conversation with them, they will try to make you feel that you are making a big deal out of nothing. They will tell you that your emotions are all over the place and that you should learn to keep them in check. As a direct result of all this, you will slowly start thinking about whether your feelings are justified or not.

You will often find the manipulator pointing out to you that the way you are dictating the events of the past is not the way they happened. When this happens, you will automatically start questioning your own memory. The manipulator does that so that they can change the narration of the past event to their own benefit.

When you have a manipulator in your circle who is gaslighting you, you will automatically find yourself apologizing way too much. Whenever there is a confrontation or an argument, you will feel the need to say sorry even though you were not the one at fault.

You will find that your well-wishers, friends, or family might not like the manipulator, and you will incessantly want to defend that person in front of others. When you can't make them understand, you will start hiding things about the manipulator and paint the best picture possible in front of your acquaintances. But you are already aware of how unacceptable the behavior of the manipulator is, but somehow you are ashamed of it, and so you don't want to reveal the details.

Gradually, after a certain point of time, you might even start feeling that something is definitely wrong with you, or you might have started to become crazy. If you are in a relationship with the manipulator, then you might also feel that it is because of you that the relationship is in tatters and that you are never going to be enough.

The manipulator will make you doubt and second-guess yourself at every stage of your life, and you become so confused that you start to trust the judgment of others more than yours. You will also falter when it comes to making decisions because you are no longer sure about your own judgment.

You will no longer be the confident person you were before. Even though you have a gut feeling about the person manipulating you, you will not speak up about it because you are afraid or are facing self-doubt about this as well.

THEY USE SARCASM TO DEVALUE YOU

Manipulators will often try to devalue you, and they do this with the help of sarcasm. Like I told you before, manipulators don't know how they can engage in direct communication, and so, they use different tactics to get what they want, and undermining and insulting the person with sarcasm is one of them. With these sarcastic comments, they will make you feel as if you don't have any feelings or that your actions don't matter at all. The aim of the manipulator is to make you feel that you are inferior, and they want to put you in a position where you feel inferior.

One very common example that shows how sarcasm is used in manipulation is when someone sends you a message that seems friendly at a glance. But if you read between the lines, you will find there is aggressive content that is meant to insult you. For example, "If you only went to a prestigious university, today you would have been living the life of your dreams." So, by saying this, they are trying to say that you are not successful and you don't lead a quality life because you are not educated enough.

When someone has been manipulated for too long, they fail to recognize this kind of behavior as manipulation. It is because they think that the other person actually has their best interests in mind, and so they are trying to help them out. But what you need to understand is that making you feel bad about yourself is not the way of helping you. It is insulting, and it will only push you further into a cycle of self-loathing. If someone wants to give you some useful advice, then they will engage in direct communication, and they won't be devaluing you. Making jokes that are insulting and make you feel inferior is not a way of showing respect.

THE 8 TRAITS THAT MAKE A PERSON EASY TO MANIPULATE

There are certain characteristics and behavioral traits that make people more vulnerable to manipulation, and people with dark psychology traits know this full well. They tend to seek out victims who have those specific behavioral traits because they are essentially easy targets. Let's talk about the traits of the favorite victims of manipulators.

EMOTIONAL INSECURITY AND FRAGILITY

Manipulators like to target victims who are emotionally insecure or emotionally fragile. Unfortunately for these victims, such traits are very easy to identify even in total strangers, so it's easy for experienced manipulators to find them.

People who are emotionally insecure tend to be very defensive when they are attacked or when they are under pressure, and that makes them easy to spot in social situations. Even after just a few interactions, a manipulator can gauge with a certain degree of accuracy, how insecure a person is. They'll try to provoke their potential targets in a subtle way, and then wait to see how the targets react. If they are overly defensive, manipulators will take it as a sign of insecurity, and they will intensify their manipulative attacks.

Manipulators can also tell if a target is emotionally insecure if he/she redirects accusations or negative comments. They will find a way to put you on the spot, and if you try to throw it back at them, or to make excuses instead of confronting the situation head-on, the manipulator could conclude that you are insecure and therefore an easy target.

People who have social anxiety also tend to have emotional insecurity, and manipulators are aware of this fact. In social gatherings, they can easily spot individuals who have social anxiety, then target them for manipulation. "Pickup artists" are able to identify the girls who seem uneasy in social situations by the way they conduct themselves. Social anxiety is difficult to conceal, especially to manipulators who are experienced at preying on emotional vulnerability.

Emotional fragility is different from emotional insecurity. Emotionally insecure people tend to show it all the time, while emotionally fragile people appear to be normal, but they break down emotionally at the slightest provocation. Manipulators like targeting emotionally fragile people because it's very easy to elicit a reaction from them. Once a manipulator finds out that you are emotionally fragile, he is going to jump at the chance to manipulate you because he knows it would be fairly easy.

Emotional fragility can be temporary, so people with these traits are often targeted by opportunistic manipulators. A person may be emotionally stable most of the time, but he/she may experience emotional fragility when they are going through a breakup, when they are grieving, or when they are dealing with a situation that is emotionally draining. The more diabolical manipulators can earn your trust, bid their time and wait for you to be emotionally fragile. Alternatively, they can use underhanded methods to induce emotional fragility in a person they are targeting.

SENSITIVE PEOPLE

Highly sensitive people are those individuals who process information at a deeper level and are more aware of the subtleties in social dynamics. They have lots of positive attributes because they tend to be very considerate of others, and they watch their step to avoid causing people any harm, whether directly or indirectly. Such people tend to dislike any form of violence or cruelty, and they are easily upset by news reports about disastrous occurrences, or even depictions of gory scenes in movies.

Sensitive people also tend to get emotionally exhausted from taking in other people's feelings. When they walk into a room, they have the immediate ability to detect other people's moods, because they are naturally skilled at identifying and interpreting other people's body language cues, facial expressions and tonal variations.

Manipulators like to target sensitive people because they are easy to manipulate. If you are sensitive to certain things, manipulators can use them against you. They will feign certain emotions to draw sensitive people in so that they can exploit them.

Sensitive people also tend to scare easily. They have a heightened "startle reflex," which means that they are more likely to show clear signs of fear or nervousness in potentially threatening situations. For example, sensitive people are more likely to jump up when someone sneaks up on them, even before they determine whether they are in any real danger. If you are a sensitive person, this trait can be very difficult to hide, and malicious people will be able to see it from a mile away.

Sensitive people also tend to be withdrawn. They are mostly introverts, and they like to keep to themselves because social stimulation can be emotionally draining for them. Manipulators who are looking to control others are more likely to target people who are introverted because that trait makes it easy to isolate potential victims.

Manipulators can also identify sensitive people by listening to how they talk. Sensitive people tend to be very proper; they never use vulgar language, and they tend to be very politically correct because they are trying to avoid offending anyone. They also tend to be polite, and they say please and thank you more often than others. Manipulators go after such people because they know that they are too polite to dismiss them right away; sensitive people will indulge anyone because they don't want to be rude, and that gives malicious people a way in.

Empathetic

giving *emphasis;* *forceful &* *clear;* *urgent*

EMPHATIC PEOPLE

Emphatic people are generally similar to highly sensitive people, except that they are more attuned to the feelings of others and the energy of the world around them. They tend to internalize other people's suffering to the point that it becomes their own. In fact, for some of them, it can be difficult to distinguish someone's discomfort from their own. Emphatic people make the best partners because they feel everything you feel. However, this makes them particularly easy to manipulate, which is why malicious people like to target them.

Malicious people can feign certain emotions, and convey those emotions to emphatic people, who will feel them as though they were real. That opens them up for exploitation. Emphatic people are the favorite targets of psychopathic conmen because they feel so deeply for others. A conman can make up stories about financial difficulties and swindle lots of money from emphatic people.

The problem with being emphatic is that because you have such strong emotions, you easily dismiss your own doubts about people because you would much rather offer help to a person who turns out to be a lair than deny help to a person who turns out to be telling the truth.

Emphatic people have a big-hearts, and they tend to be extremely generous, often to their own detriment. They are highly charitable, and they feel guilty when others around them suffer, even if it's not their fault and they can't do anything about it. Malicious people have a very easy time taking such people on guilt trips. They are the kind of people who would willingly fork over their life savings to help their friends get out of debt, even if it means they would be ruined financially.

Malicious people like to get into relationships with emphatic people because they are easy to take advantage of. Emphatic people try to avoid getting into intimate relationships in the first place because they know that it's easy for them to get engulfed in such relationships and to lose their identities in the process. However, manipulators will doggedly pursue them because they know that once they get it, they can guilt the emphatic person into doing anything they want.

Empathetic

FEAR OF LONELINESS

Many people are afraid of being alone, but this fear is more heightened in a small percentage of the population. This kind of fear can be truly paralyzing for those who experience it, and it can open them up to exploitation by malicious people. For example, there are many people who stay in dysfunctional relationships because they are afraid they will never find someone else to love them if they break up with an abusive partner. Manipulators can identify this fear in a victim, and they'll often do everything they can to fuel it further to make sure that the person is crippled by it. People who are afraid of being alone can tolerate or even rationalize any kind of abuse.

The fear of being alone can be easy to spot in a potential victim. People with this kind of fear tend to exude some level of desperation at the beginning of relationships, and they can sometimes come across as clingy. While ordinary people may think of being clingy as a red flag, manipulative people will see it as an opportunity to exploit somebody. If you are attached to them, they'll use manipulative techniques to make you even more dependent on them. They can withhold love and affection (e.g., by using the silent treatment) to make the victim fear that he/she is about to get dumped so that they act out of desperation and cede more control to the manipulator.

The fear of being alone is, for the most part, a social construct, and it disproportionately affects women more than men. For generations, our society has taught women that their goal in life is to get married and have children, so, even the more progressive women who reject this social construct are still plagued by social pressures to adhere to those old standards. That being said, the fact is that men also tend to be afraid of being alone.

People with abandonment issues stemming from childhood tend to experience the fear of loneliness to a higher degree. There are also those people who may not necessarily fear loneliness in general, but they are afraid of being separated from the important people in their lives. For example, lots of people end up staying in abusive or dysfunctional relationships because they are afraid of being separated from their children.

FEAR OF DISAPPOINTING OTHERS

We all feel a certain sense of obligation towards the people in our lives, but there are some people who are extremely afraid of disappointing others. This kind of fear is similar to the fear of embarrassment and the fear of rejection because it means that the person puts a lot of stock into how others perceive him or her. The fear of disappointing others can occur naturally, and it can actually be useful in some situations; parents who are afraid of disappointing their families will work harder to provide for them, and children who are afraid of disappointing their parents will study harder at school. In this case, the fear is actually constructive. However, it becomes unhealthy when it's directed at the wrong people, or when it forces you to compromise your own comfort and happiness.

When manipulators find out that you have a fear of disappointing others, they'll try to put you in a position where you feel like you owe them something. They'll do certain favors for you and then they'll manipulate you into believing that you have a sense of obligation towards them. They will then guilt you into complying with any request whenever they want something from you.

PERSONALITY DEPENDENT DISORDERS AND EMOTIONAL DEPENDENCY

Dependent personality disorder refers to a real disorder that is characterized by a person having an excessive and even pervasive need to be taken care of. This need often leads the person to be submissive towards the people in their lives and to be clingy and afraid of separation. People with this disorder act in ways that are meant to elicit caregiving. They tend to practice what's called "learned helplessness." This is where they act out of a conviction that they are unable to do certain things for themselves and they need the help of others.

Such people have a hard time making decisions, even when dealing with simple things like picking out which clothes to wear. They need constant reassurance and advice, and they let others take the lead in their own lives. These are the kinds of people who either move back into their parents' homes as adults or treat their spouses and partners as though they are their parents.

Manipulators like to target people with dependent personality disorders because they are very easy to control and dominate. These people willingly cede control over their lives to others, so when manipulators come knocking, they don't face much resistance. Manipulators start off by giving them a false sense of security, but once they have won their trust, they switch gears and start imposing their will on them.

Emotional dependency is somewhat similar to dependent personality disorder, but it doesn't rise to the level of clinical significance. It stems from having low self-esteem, and it's often a result of childhood abandonment issues. People with an emotional dependency will play the submissive role in relationships for fear of losing their partners. They tend to be very agreeable because they want to please the people in their lives. Such people are easy to manipulate and malicious people can easily dominate them.

14 MANIPULATION TACTICS

REVERSE PSYCHOLOGY

The first tactic that a dark persuader can use is reverse psychology. This technique consists in assuming a behavior opposite to the desired one, with the expectation that this "prohibition" will arouse curiosity and therefore induce the person to do what is really desired.

Some people are known to be like boomerangs because they refuse to go in the direction that they are sent to but take the opposite route. It works better when someone else is educated and chooses instinctively rather than thinking about things. They can introduce the intention to do X thing when they suggest the "do not do X." When you claim that you will do it, you may wonder whether you will do so.

A dark persuader can use this type of behavior because it is a weakness that the victim has. Take an example of a friend who loves to eat junk food at any opportunity he gets. The dark persuader knows this and therefore will suggest that they should eat healthy because it will be good for him, knowing that the friend will choose fast food, anyway.

Reverse Psychology can be used in sales techniques when dealing with a difficult customer.

The seller, in this case, can say: "this is a product for rich people, I don't know if it can work for you because it costs a lot of money". So, the seller is like saying: "I don't want to sell it to you, it's not the right product for you because you can't afford it", just because reverse psychology leads the person to want the product even more.

MASKING TRUE INTENTIONS (DOOR IN THE FACE)

Masking true intentions is another tactic a dark persuader will use to get what they want. A dark persuader will disguise their true intentions from their victims and can use different approaches depending on their victims and the surrounding circumstance. One approach a dark persuader can use is using two requests consecutively because people find it hard to refuse two requests in a row. Take this example; a manipulator wants $500 from their victim. The dark persuader will begin by explaining why they need $1000 while stating what will happen if they are not able to come up with that amount. The victim may feel guilt or compassion but will kindly explain to the manipulator that they cannot lend the amount because, quite frankly, it's more than they can manage to give. This is when the persuader will lessen the amount to $500, which was what they wanted from the beginning. They will attach the amount with some emotional reason where the victim will be unable to refuse the second request. The dark persuader walks away with the original sum, and the victim is left confused about what took place.

FOOT IN THE DOOR

This tactic is implemented in increments. This begins with the manipulator asking for small favors. Every time the victim complies, the manipulator will ask for increasingly bigger favors until they get what they ultimately want, or they exhaust their victim. At that point, the manipulator needs to move on to a fresh victim.

Consider this example:

A manipulator wants a large sum of money. Yet, they know they won't get it if they just ask for it. So, they ask for a tiny sum. Then, they pay it back. Next, they ask for a bigger sum and then pay it back. They do this as they build up trust capital until one day; they get what they want, never to be heard from again.

This example clarifies why this technique is called put your "foot in the door" and make room with your whole body.

A more rudimentary approach consists in asking multiple people for money with no intention of paying it back. Eventually, they exhaust the people around them. So, they need to move on and find new victims.

THE BLAME GAME

If the manipulator wants to make you do something against your will, he will have a better chance of getting that behavior by making you feel guilty. Blame is one of the most powerful manipulation techniques known to mankind. Guilt can be used to manipulate people by making them feel inferior to the help and support they have received, or it can also be used to make others feel inadequate for a "condition" they have. Think about all those times you hear people say, "things would be different if I wasn't sick." This is one of the most rudimentary ways to make someone feel guilty, but it is very powerful. Besides, you might hear others say things like, "remember when you need my help? Now I need your help." This is a clear attempt to convince someone to follow the manipulator's intentions.

PUTTING THE OTHER PERSON DOWN

Through this technique, we try to make the other person feel less capable than he is. For example, you find every pretext to point out to the victim when makes a mistake, and you do it repeatedly, to throw off his self-esteem. A person with low self-esteem is manageable and controllable, therefore manipulable. This way, the manipulator will feel in control of the situation.

When a person tries to manipulate you with this technique, remember that they will attack your identity, so they will tell you phrases like "you are incapable" instead, they will never tell you "You are behaving like an incapable person." To react to this technique, you have to detach yourself from this psycho-trap and think that instead, the person is judging your behavior at that moment and not your identity.

LEADING QUESTIONS

This involves the dark persuader questions that trigger some response from the victim. A persuader may ask a question like, "do you think that this person could be so mean?" This question implies that the person will be bad in one way or another. An example of a non-leading question is, "What do you think about that person?" When they use leading questions, dark persuaders ensure that they use them carefully. Dark persuaders know that when the victim feels like they are being led in order to trigger a certain response from them, they will become more resistant to being persuaded. When the dark persuader gets a feeling that the victim has to be aware, that he or she is being led, they will immediately change tactics and return to asking the leading questions only when the victim has come down.

FATIGUE INDUCEMENT

The impacts of mental fatigue on perceptual, emotional and motivational factors are complex. Special effects, in the case of exhaustion, can be assumed to rely on the essence of the operation that causes fatigue. This study investigated the impact of exhaustion due to different activities based on working memory demands on brain function and efficiency. The results showed that driving quality was not impaired by exhaustion. The effects of fatigue on novelty therapy depended on the mental requirements for the task that caused fatigue.

CREATING AN ILLUSION

Create exaggeratedly high or unrealizable expectations, but presenting and selling them in such a powerful, persuasive and tempting way for you that you'll end up believing it.

With this technique, it is possible to make the victim see the most beautiful future in such a way that she will be willing to do anything to make it happen, even spend a lot of money. The goal is to make people "daydream" to give them the hope of living their lives to the full.

COMMITMENT AND CONGRUITY

Highly skilled and sophisticated manipulators know that building trust capital is essential, especially when seeking to build a long-term approach. Think about the most sophisticated conmen you can imagine. These are individuals who take time, often years, building up trust around them through congruent behavior so that others can fall into their trap.

At first, no one suspects the least bit in this individual as they have earned everyone's trust. As they gain more and more trust, they can use that trust capital to deceive others. This gives them some leeway in case they slip up. Given their track record, they will always have the benefit of the doubt.

This tactic is not common in less-sophisticated manipulators as it requires a great deal of dedication. Impulsive individuals will never be able to pull this off as they focus more on short-term rather than long-term gain. Through this type of tactic, many manipulators are able to build a name for themselves in their chose domain. However, they are often exposed. When this occurs, the world is shocked to learn that who they thought was a pillar of their community was actually a manipulator.

One good example of this is a cheating spouse. An individual may cheat on their spouse for years without them noticing what's going on. Then, one day, the manipulator makes a mistake, whatever it is, and they are exposed. The shock that comes to the victim is overwhelming.

The reason why this tactic always backfires is due to the fact that the manipulator doesn't know when to stop. The longer they go without getting caught, the more they think the con will last forever. History has taught us that everyone gets caught eventually.

RECIPROCITY

This is the classic "quid pro quo," in other words; you scratch my back, I'll scratch yours. However, the victim doesn't know the extent to which they are being manipulated.

A great example of this can be found with informants.

When a manipulator wishes to extract information from someone, they may offer tidbits of information of their own in the hopes of motivating the victim to furnish the information the manipulator is looking for. However, the key to making this tactic work is that the manipulator must give information of little or no value while extracting information that may be profitable.

Manipulators also use this tactic when doing favors. They build up capital and then "call-in" favors.

While this may seem like it's perfectly reasonable, it is a manipulation tactic as the manipulator doesn't do favors out of the goodness of their heart. They do it so that they can have people they can rely on in times of need. Alternatively, they can resort to guilt, or even blackmail, if the other party refuses to cooperate.

SCARCITY AND DEMAND

Often, manipulators realize that they have something, or at least have access to something, that people really want. When this occurs, they are able to manipulate those around them by creating a false illusion of scarcity.

Earlier, we talked about how advertisers generally use phrases such as "limited quantities available" or "while supplies last." These phrases have become so cliché that no one really buys into them anymore.

Yet, manipulators can make this work by creating a sense that there really is a scarcity of a product or service. Some of the more outright, devious ways of pulling this off are by planting fake informants who spread lies. When these lies spread, people may begin to panic and flock to get the products and services in question.

Another way of pulling this off is by spreading rumors on social media. Some people fall for it, and some don't. In the end, the goal is to create enough confusion so that no one is able to tell the difference.

Lastly, manufacturers may go as far as hoarding supplies in order to create an artificial scarcity. This has worked well throughout history. In fact, it's worked so well that it is illegal in most countries. Still, manufacturers can pull this off by controlling the entire supply chain of their products. So, any disruption along that line will cause scarcity thereby creating panic in people. The manufacturers themselves are not responsible for the scarcity as they are not the ones who technically caused the issue.

CONSENSUS

This tactic consists in setting situations in such a manner that people will agree to them regardless of what it is. Governments do this all the time. For instance, they know that no one will ever agree to a tax hike. Yet, they frame the situation in such a manner that if people wish to continue receiving government benefits, they need to accept the tax hike as there is no other way to fund it. So, people reluctantly accept the tax hike out of fear of losing their benefits.

A similar approach occurs during elections. This tactic is employed when voters go for the "least of the worst," that is, they realize that none of the candidates are actually good. But they'll vote for the candidate who isn't the worst.

In the end, this tactic is like "choosing your poison."

BIAS

Bias refers to people's prejudices and presuppositions. People always have an opinion about one thing or another. So, manipulators exploit this to their benefit. For example, political candidates run on a specific platform in their district because they know that that's what people want to hear.

On the other hand, you may find manipulators playing off people's fears. For example, a supervisor in a factory knows that people in that town are fearful of losing their jobs. As a result, the workers are reluctant to accept any changes that the company wants to make. This is especially important to the supervisor as they are afraid of losing their own job. So, the supervisor uses the factory workers as pawns in their scheme.

EMOTIONAL BLACKMAIL

This is where the manipulator acts to generate empathy or guilt in the subject they are manipulating. These emotions are chosen because they are the two most powerful human emotions and are the most likely to steer others to do what the manipulator wants. The manipulator is able to exploit their subject, using their empathy or guilt, to compel others to comply or to help them achieve their ultimate goal.

Oftentimes, the manipulator cannot only produce these feelings but can cause certain degrees of empathy or guilt, which are out of proportion to the situation. This means that they can take a situation—

for example, bailing out at a party—to seem like one is missing out on a wedding or funeral.

Emotional blackmail is but one of the manipulators' techniques.

THE 6+1 WEAPONS OF PERSUASION

There are many times when the human mind is pretty easy to influence, but it does take a certain set of skills to get people to stop and listen to you. Not everyone is good with influence and persuasion, though. They can talk all day and would not be able to convince others to do what they want. On the other hand, there are those who could persuade anyone to do what they want, even if they had just met this person for the first time. Knowing how to work with these skills will make it easier for you to recognize a manipulator and be better prepared to avoid them if needed.

The first thing that we need to look at is what persuasion is. Persuasion is simply the process or action taken by a person or a group of people when they want to cause something to change. This could be in relation to another human being and something that changes in their inner mental systems or their external behavior patterns.

The act of persuasion, when it is done in the proper way, can sometimes create something new within the person, or it can just modify something that is already present in their minds. There are actually three different parts that come with the process of persuasion including:

- The communicator or other source of the persuasion
- The persuasive nature of the appeal
- The audience or the target person of the appeal

It is important that all three elements are taken into consideration before you try to do any form of persuasion on your own. You can just look around at the people who are in your life, and you will probably be able to see some types of persuasion happening all over the place.

Experts say that people who are good leaders and who have good persuasion powers will utilize the following techniques to help them be successful:

- Exchanging
- Stating
- Legitimizing
- Logical persuasion

- Appealing to value
- Modeling
- Alliance building
- Consulting
- Socializing
- Appealing to a relationship

The above options are all positive ways in which you can use persuasion to your advantage. Most people will be amenable to these happening. But on the other side, there are four negative tactics of persuasion that you can do as well. These would include options like manipulating, avoiding, intimidating and threatening. These negative tactics will be easier for the target to recognize, which is why most manipulators will avoid using them if possible.

Now, you can use some of the tactics above, but according to psychologist Robert Cialdini, there are six major principles of persuasion that can help you to get the results that you want without the target being able to notice what is going on. Let us take a look at these six weapons and how they can be effective.

THE SIX + ONE WEAPONS OF PERSUASION

Reciprocity

The first principle of persuasion that you can use is known as reciprocity. This is based on the idea that when you offer something to someone, they will feel a bit indebted to you and will want to reciprocate it back. Humans are wired to be this way to survive. For the manipulator to use this option, they will make sure that they are doing some kind of favor for their target. Whether that is paying them some compliments, giving them a ride to work, helping out with a big project, or getting them out of trouble. Once the favor is done, the target will feel like they owe a debt to the manipulator. The manipulator will then be able to ask for something, and it will be really hard for the target to say no.

Commitment And Consistency

It is in the nature of humans to settle for what is already tried and tested in the mind. Most of us have a mental image of who we are and how things should be. And most people are not going to be willing to experiment, so they will keep on acting the way that they did in the past. So, to get them to work with this principle and do what you want, you first need to get them to commit to something. The steps that you would need to follow to get your target to do what you want through commitment and consistency include:

- Start out with something small. You can ask the target to do something small, something that is easier to manage the change before they start to integrate it more into their personality and get hooked on the habit.
- You can get the target to accept something publicly so that they will feel more obligated to see it through.
- Reward the target when they can stick to the course. Rewards will be able to help strengthen the interest of the target in the course of action that you want them to do.

Social Proof

This is another one that will rely on the human tendency, and it relies on the fact that people place a lot of value and trust in other people and in their opinions on things that we have not tried yet. This can be truer if the information comes from a close friend or a person who is perceived as the expert. It is impossible to try out everything in life, and having to rely on others can put us at a disadvantage. This means that we need to find a reliable source to help us get started. A manipulator may be able to get someone to do something by acting as a close friend or an expert. They are able to get the target to try out a course of action because they have positioned themselves as the one who knows the most about the situation or the action.

Likeability

We all know that it is easy to feel attracted to a certain set of people. This can extend to friends and family members as well. So, if you would like to get others to like you and be open to persuasion from you, you first need to figure out how to go from an acquaintance to a friend. This will work similarly to the reciprocity that we talked about earlier, but some of the basic steps that you will need to follow to make this work include:

- The attraction phase: You need to make sure that there is something about you that instantly draws the other person to you.
- Make yourself relatable: People are more likely to be drawn to you if you are relatable to them in some way. It

is also easier to influence another person if they consider you their friend.

- Communicate like a friend: Even if the two of you are not quite friends yet, you will be able to make use of the right communication skills so that the target will associate you as a friend.
- Make it look like you are both in the same groups and that you are fighting for the same causes: This can make it easier to establish a rapport with them.

Authority

If you want to make sure that you can influence another person, then you need to dress and act the part. This means that you should wear clothes, as well as accessories, that will help you look like you are the one in command. Some of the ways that you can do this include:

- Wear clothes that are befitting to what people will perceive an authoritative figure would wear.
- When you communicate with the target, you need to do so in a commanding fashion.
- Make sure that you can use the lexicon and the language of experts in that field.

When you can position yourself as the authority figure, people will look to you for the answers that they need. It does not matter how well they know you or not. You will have a great opportunity to influence them the way that you want them to behave.

Scarcity

The last weapon that you can use for persuasion is known as scarcity. Humans like the idea of being exclusive and are drawn to anything that they are not necessarily able to find anywhere else. When you make something exclusive, you have a chance of making it appear more valuable. People are also going to become fearful when something they desire starts to disappear. This whole idea is part of the supply and demand principle. If you have something that is abundant, then it will be perceived as having a lower value and cheap. But if it is rare, then it must have a higher value and be more expensive.

This can work for human beings and for products in the same way. Some things that you should keep in mind when you want to use the scarcity principle with persuasion include:

- Always imply that the thing you are offering is not going to be available to the target anywhere else.
- If you can, it is a good idea to implement a countdown timer on what you are offering. This gives a physical indicator to the target that what you are offering is truly going to disappear.
- You should never go back on the stipulations that you said in the beginning. You need to make sure that the target knows that what you offered is scarce, or this method is not going to work very well.

All of these principles can be effective ways for you to be able to use persuasion to manipulate your target. It is important to learn how to use them all and to do so in a covert way so that your target is not able to realize what you are doing.

When you are successful with bringing all of this together, you are sure to get the results that you want each time.

Unity

Unity is the art of making people feel like they belong to a group. The manipulator will see their goal, and they will make sure to link it with one of the target's desires. Then, the manipulator will make sure to show that they value those desires. Whether it's through humor, entertainment, or anything else, the target will feel unified with the manipulator and will want to keep up that relationship. Once they're feeling this way, it will be very hard for them to defy whatever the manipulator wants them to do.

Unity appeals to needs, desires and values we all share. If you can understand what these are for your target, you will be able to connect with them. However, when using this tactic, it is incredibly important that you are being honest with the person.

5 WAYS TO PROTECT YOURSELF FROM DARK PSYCHOLOGY AND MANIPULATION

There are so many things that you can do to protect yourself from the manipulation that you feel from another person.

FIRST, YOU NEED TO AVOID BLAMING YOURSELF FOR THE SITUATION

The manipulator is never going to be one who will admit that they did something wrong. It is their job to feel as good as possible, and they will go through and make sure that you feel inadequate. In order to help them get what they want out of life, the manipulator is going to work hard to make you feel guilty and bad about yourself and everything.

During this time, remember that you do deserve to be loved and have dreams and goals. Remember that the other person, the manipulator, is trying to deceive you and make you feel bad, and they are not providing you with the respect that you deserve. You need to be able to stand up for yourself and fight off against this to get the results that you want.

Manipulators are often going to twist and change the facts because this helps them to come out the winner and come out ahead of everyone else. When you are responding to this distortion of facts, it is vital to seek out some clarification. Explain to them, firmly but respectfully, that you don't remember the facts that way, and that you want to try and understand what is going on. Being able to ask some questions can make a lot of difference.

LEARNING HOW TO LISTEN TO YOURSELF IS GOING TO HELP AS WELL

Think about the way you feel about the situation at hand. Do you feel like you are free and happy, or do you feel like you are pressured and obliged to do things for someone when they ask? Does it seem like the other person is impacting you all of the time, and it is all going to be a big inconvenience to do the action for them, even though you have never wanted to do it? The answers that you can give to this are going to serve as a guide to where this particular relationship is heading, and if it is a good one for you to still be in.

You can also work to curtail some of the guilt trips that the other person is sending your way. This one is hard to work with, but if you can approach this, and not let the other person determine the situation and make the interpretation, then you will find that it is so much easier. You have to be able to take the words that the manipulator has said to you and let them know that they are unkind, unrealistic, inconsiderate and dis-respectful to you along the way. Some examples of do-ing this will be below:

Yes, I know that right now, you are having some troubles. But it is not my responsibility to deal with this. I am not available after a certain time, and it is im-portant that you call someone else if you think you need help. I know right now; you are going through quite a bit in your personal life. But this doesn't change the fact that I need to go to work, class and other obli-gations. Maybe it is better you talk with another person on some occasions, or even consider some of the re-sources that I have sent you on mental health instead.

I do care a lot about the hard work you have put in, and how you have been able to help me. I've said that many times in the past. The problem right now is that you are not showing enough appreciation for how much I do care about you.

YOU CAN ALSO LEARN HOW TO FOCUS ALL OF THE ATTENTION BACK ON THE PERSON WHO IS TRYING TO MANIPULATE YOU

Instead of allowing that person to ask you questions and be the one in control of the demands, you can take control over the situation that is there, and then turn it back on them. Any time you feel that they are pressured to do something that seems unreasonable, or you are not comfortable with, then you can ask them some questions that will turn things back on them.

And always remember that when you are dealing with a manipulator, you should never jump right into a quick decision without having the time to think it through. The manipulator knows that when their victim has to make some swift decisions, then they are going to end up making decisions that are not always in their best interest. Instead of just giving in and agreeing to it, it is much better if you can first tell the other person that you will think about it.

Of course, this is probably going to make the manipulator a bit mad at you for what they are doing. They want you to make that decision quickly because they know that if you have the time to think it over, you are going to say no, and not help them out with it. This means that if you ever feel like there is a lot of pressure that comes here, it is going to be a sign that someone is trying to manipulate you a little bit.

YOU MAY FIND THAT THIS IS THE PERFECT TIME TO FIND YOUR SUPPORT GROUP

Sometimes, a manipulator is going to try and isolate you from other people. This is because they feel that if they can get you alone, they will be able to convince you to do more things that you normally would not. If you focus on some of the healthier relationships in your life, and even start to build up some new ones, you will feel more happiness and confidence in the process. You can look at new friends, old friends, mentors, family members and more. These are great to have because they are the ones who will help you keep the balance and happiness that is needed. And when that starts to show up more in your life, the hold that the manipulator is going to have over you will be gone.

AND FINALLY, IT IS OFTEN A GOOD IDEA TO STAY AWAY FROM THE MANIPULATOR

If you find that it is harmful or at least difficult to interact with a specific person, it is time to distance yourself a bit more. Remember that your happiness, as long as it is not harming anyone else, is what is important, and it is never your job to go in and change the other person. If you find that the manipulator is someone you have to be around regularly, like a coworker or someone in your family, try to see if there are ways that you can safely and effectively limit the interactions that you have with them. It is best to only engage with that person when it is necessary.

Now, when you do try to separate from the manipulator, remember that they are not going to like this and they are likely going to try and use all of the tools and techniques that they have at their exposure to help try to get you to stay. This means that when you do this, be prepared for the victim card, the smear campaigns, the guilt trips and more. This is done because the manipulator is starting to see that they are no longer holding that control over you and they do not like it. If you can hold out for a bit, rather than running right back, then you will be the one who wins.

14 COVERT MANIPULATIVE TACTICS

Overt aggression, such as subtle abuse, criticism and narcissistic abuse, comes in manipulation. While the most favorite covert arms of a manipulator are lying, guilt, complaining, denying, comparing, pretending innocence or ignorance, bribery, blaming, assumptions, mind games, undermining, blackmailing, faking concerns, gifting and flattering.

Typical techniques used by manipulators are given here:

INTIMIDATION

It is not necessary that intimidation comes with direct threats. Sometimes, it is subtle. A specific statement, tone, or look can also intimidate the victim. "I always get what I want" is one statement of light intimidation.

"I have friends at higher ranks," "No one is irreplaceable," "You are not so young anymore" and so on.

Another intimidation strategy is to concoct a story to make you feel fearful. "He left his wife and kids, house and everything else."

LYING

Lying is one of the most common tools of manipulators. Such people lie because they want to achieve their dream/target. They give (false) excuses to others or try to hide what their mind says.

Vague answers and questions are also a form of lies. Hiding some information and highlighting only a part of the information is also another type.

There are many examples of white lies that people say to manipulate others. But some of the most common and obvious examples from advertisement and brand marketing are: "Customer is king," "100 percent pure product," "Fresh food" and "Chemical-free," etcetera.

AVOIDANCE

Most manipulators want to avoid difficult situations and take responsibility. They also want to avoid discussions on their behaviors (fearing confrontation). Such people can put you on the defensive, saying, "you are always pinpointing me."

Sometimes, avoidance can be subtle, too. How to know somebody is avoiding a discussion? When they subtly try to shift the topic or get up from their seats to move out.

DENIAL

Denial is also a bad tactic. Not realizing that one has an addiction or a bad habit, denying to accept the reality and avoiding certain situations are some of its examples.

Denial can both be conscious and unconscious. An example of conscious denial is disclaiming knowledge of behavior, agreements and promises. It also includes rationalization and excuses.

Usually, manipulators act as if the victim is making a big deal at a loss. They also excuse the victim's actions to make people doubtful about themselves or create a soft corner in your heart.

GUILT, SHAME AND BLAME

Have you noticed politicians and entertainment celebrities blaming and shaming each other? One of the classic examples of blaming is this political statement: "The preceding government did not do anything, and that's why this issue occurred."

Manipulators accuse others usually. Their belief is "the best defense is a good offense." Doing this (shifting the blame) makes the other person feel guilty and ashamed. This is a tactic used everywhere, let alone in politics, media and courts.

Blaming is a must weapon of abusers. Addicts also blame others for their bad habits. Criminal defendants also like putting the blame on others.

In most domestic violence cases, culprits put the blame on the victims for their violent acts. One of the examples is from South Africa. I am using fake names for the couple. Let's say the husband's name was "Isaac" and the wife was called "Anna." They had four children together. The husband was a farmer and his wife was a maid.

Isaac used to beat his wife every day. The list of reasons he gave for beating up his wife was ridiculous. He listed issues like:

- The food was uncooked
- The coffee was cold
- The dress his wife pressed was not clean
- His chair was dusty, and so on.

Now you might think, why do people like to shift the blame? Just to feel superior and in control!!! Shaming is another tactic associated with blaming and guilt. People shame others to make them feel inferior or demean them. And comparing is a subtle but highly effective (for the manipulators) form of shaming.

You must have seen many examples of shaming and comparisons in real life. One of the most common examples is, "Your sister/brother took more marks than you. If you had studied harder, you could also secure better marks than your sister/brother."

Another popular example is the tagline, "Like father, like son," when used sarcastically. This is done to make others feel bad and, yes, inferior.

PLAYING OTHERS

Playing with others is something really dangerous. Sometimes, people threaten their spouses that they will commit suicide if the spouse leaves them. This is just a tactic to make the partner stay. Instilling the feeling of guilt and sympathy to gain what you want is a type of "play."

Many fundraising organizations and (sorry to mention) beggars attempt to gain sympathy. Have you ever read a note or letter from a fundraising organization? They write like this:

"We are raising funds for an orphanage. We want to educate small orphans. The money you send us will be used to provide the little innocent children with food, books and some clothes. Help us because we are doing something good."

Once I met a beggar on a trip to India. The women were in shabby condition. She had a small, very weak baby and a stick in her hands. She was wearing a bandage on her left leg and had a broken feeder in her pocket. I was with a friend who knew Hindi. She translated her story to me, and I was about to break into tears. Because the story was actually heart-breaking:

"I am all alone in this world. I have no one but this baby. He is my world, but yesterday, the doctor told me the baby has a tumor. We need to operate on her soon, or she will die within six months. I am so helpless and homeless. If you do not help me, I might also die before the baby."

Did you know what my reaction was? I opened my purse and gave some money to her. When we came back to the hotel, our guide told us that the beggar we met on the way was a professional and the baby she had was "rented out" for a day. The woman pays for rent on a daily basis (Darlene Lancer, 2019).

CHARMING, LOVE BOMBING AND GIFTING

Who does not like charming personalities? Don't we get attracted to them? Well, manipulators know this. This is why many of them try this tactic to get their way.

Many movies show that the heroine or hero of the film dresses up nicely, wears makeup and makes special preparations to meet with a person they want to attract. Sometimes, it is the villain that the heroine wants to attract by posing charming to him. She might want to take revenge or take out the dark secret that the villain hides.

What happens then is the otherwise simple-looking and innocent heroine goes to meet with her target after coming out from a parlor. She looks entirely different and charming. Not because she wanted to look nice. But because she had a purpose in mind. She wanted to attract, manipulate and get her way!

Love bombing is another form of presenting attractions to the victim. You must have seen people giving you so many compliments and good remarks. "Oh! You look so pretty." "What dress you are wearing." "Wow! I love your hairdo..."

What are these? These are compliments to allure you, simple as that!

Flattering and buttering is also a form of manipulation. You see, many people around you do this for gain. Siblings also do that. "I really like your manners. In fact, I really like many of your habits, dear. Please, brother, get me a phone."

Sometimes, gifting is also a form of manipulation. It can help close your mouth. One classic example of gifting for this purpose is accepting gifts from males (to females) and from employees to bosses. Employees sometimes present gifts to their bosses to keep them happy. Sometimes, men also buy "gifts for her" to get what they need from her!!!!

BRIBERY AND FAVORS

Bribery is also manipulation. Here is a story. Ryan got 30 percent marks in mathematics. He showed the result to his father. His father got furious. He wanted his son to clear the subject. But he also knew that the son could not pass the mathematics exam. So, what he did was bribed the examiner to give his son good marks.

This is one example. The fact is we always bribe others to get our way. Be careful!

BLACKMAILING

Here we are talking about the subtle form of blackmailing. The one in which manipulators ask you something to do politely; otherwise, they would not do you a favor. Subtle blackmailing like, "if you do not help me in my assignment, I will tell your teacher you skipped the last class" and more.

COERCION

This is not fun. This is the use of force for your benefit. To get their way, manipulators do not stop using threats, fear and weaknesses of others. One example can be, "if you do not help me steal this money, I will tell everyone that you have an extramarital relationship with your neighbor."

This makes the victim feel that not listening to the manipulator might have some worst consequences than helping them do that.

Another very common example of this (and blackmailing) is the use of a woman's weakness to make them pose nude for the manipulators. A newspaper story made headlines in the recent past.

"A girl was asked to give her nudes to a man because she had a secret relationship with him. The man made her do "anything" for his pleasure, and if she failed to do that, the man would tell her family about their secret relationship.

SILENT TREATMENT

This happens mostly among friends and family. Spouses pose silently to make their partners feel anxious and do whatever they demand. This is a technique used to make the other person feel the urge to talk to the other person and break the silence.

REASONING

The reasoning is not manipulation, right. Sometimes, manipulators use this technique to divert your attention and make you do something. This technique is usually shown in dramas and old movies.

"Because the hero was very poor, his friend gave him a reason to rob the landlord."

ACTING SMART

You often meet people who are not smart. But they think they are really smart. To prove this, they do different things. For instance, they will give you more reasons to jog when you are already jogging.

If you are cooking something, they will join you and ask you how you made it when you tell them the recipe. This is quite possible that that person will instantly reject your recipe or cut you midway to tell their way of cooking the same thing.

> ➢ "Where did you buy this suit from?"
> ➢ "I bought it from the mall ABC."
> ➢ "Price?"
> ➢ "$150."

"Oh my…. somebody just robbed you. This does not look expensive. Its price is not more than $20. I have bought the same dress from XYZ mall for $20."

Do not pay attention to such a person. It is not necessary that he is telling you the truth. It can be a tact to make you dependent on them for shopping.

MAKING SOMEONE JEALOUS

This is also a tactic to make you (do) what a manipulative person wants you to do. "Listen! He is talking to his friend in front of you. Go ask him why he is doing that." Such statements are deliberately whispered into your ears to raise your blood pressure level. And make you fight with others.

6 ADVANTAGES AND 6 DISADVANTAGES OF DARK PSYCHOLOGY

D ark psychology comes with advantages and disadvantages together. These are the two sides of the same coin. There is nothing in the world that comes out only with advantages. The same goes for the disadvantages that there is nothing in the world that only comes with disadvantages. It is always good and bad in the situation. The same goes for dark psychology that there are some advantages and disadvantages to it.

ADVANTAGES OF DARK PSYCHOLOGY

There Is No More Fear

People have a side of themselves that they fear. They don't want it to come in front of anybody.

People take their dark side as a weakness because they fear the outcomes. Sometimes they also feel that it might overpower their personality. That's why they have issues of trust in themselves.

As a result, they put themselves down a lot of time. The Dark Side is not that dark as one thinks. It helps people to explore their weaknesses and the dark side of their personalities. Once they get hold of a dark side, they don't fear anything. Then, there is no more desire for approval seeking. Once it is out in front of the world, nothing is stopping you from achieving anything.

They Are Good Convincers

The Darker psychology side is very good at manipulating. They need to be great convincers. They need to know where to trigger a person and how to do it. Sometimes people standing for election in school and high school or general elections need to be great at convincing to get the votes. People whose dark side is a little more superior can use a plus point and convince people to vote for them. It helps them achieve what they want but not in a bad manner until they are not destroying anybody. Sometimes fighting for their position turns out to be fine if they are doing it in a boundary. It gives people good convincing powers.

It Helps Them Take Risk

There is nothing wrong with taking the risk if it is not having any bad results. A lot of people don't do a lot of things that they want to just because they are scared of the outcome especially when it comes to having fun. They experience everything in life, so the advantages of dark psychology are that since they don't say anything, they overcome their fear easily and they probably live life to its fullest. It takes everything to do the following at the right moment, so sometimes their impulsiveness helps them have more fun as compared to the people who keep on thinking about the outcomes.

It Makes Them Grow

Self-focus is not bad until it is not having any serious issues. Self-focus is very important for personal growth and personal maturity. Sometimes it helps people to focus on themselves completely and have them understand what they want in life to grow and to be a better person. It is something that helps a person to be a better person.

It Brings Out Enthusiasm

People with the opposite side of it are known as narcissists, and they are great at selling themselves. Similarly, they are great enthusiastic people because they try to be happier in situations that bring out the best results in the end.

Enthusiasm: you need to be full of energy ball for your ambitions. Enthusiasm for work is important for people. Great enthusiastic people know what they have to do in certain situations, so they are good people to work within a group.

They Are Very Precise

One of the dark psychology personality characteristics is that these people are very precise and careful. They always want to achieve much better than them. They are always looking out to work better and nice to make everything better. They are also known as perfectionists, so the probability of them making mistakes is very low. They are always trying to do something better, something that could be more appealing.

This type of person is great when it comes to achieving goals because they know what they want. They are so precious in doing everything, and it helps them succeed in life.

DISADVANTAGES OF DARK PSYCHOLOGY

They Become Paranoid

It undermines people in stressful circumstances and makes a person paranoid. Dark psychology mainly refers to the Dark Side, which causes a person to feel threatened in a lot of ways. They always keep on thinking that people are planning or working against them even though there is no truthfulness. They keep on making situations in their head that don't exist in the First Place. It happens a lot of time to a person, and sometimes people are also aware of the fact that it does not have any real basis, but still, they cannot stop themselves from feeling the fear.

It can get more severe and sometimes turns out to be a mental health condition, but the darker side of the person just makes up something that whatever is happening has the motive against them, or it is a threat to them. The feeling that there is something that is actively trying to harm them when there is no search proves.

Even if something is happening in reality and it is happening in a positive and better way, some people think that there is something in it that is not right. They bring out the negative and positive aspects together, and later it costs them.

It is the dark psychology of the person at the darker side of the person who is suppressing the positive side, and no matter how much a person wants to stop, they can't stop. They keep on building situations and thoughts. From time to time, it is not linked to anything. It is a waste. It doesn't have any benefits.

They Turn into a Harmful Manipulator

One of the things about dark psychology is that people are great manipulators. Two different things are convincing, and manipulation is two different things convincing is a good trait, whereas manipulative people are the masters of deception.

Manipulative people are not interested in any other benefits of any other damages. They only want to gain control, and they want people to be unwillingly supportive of their plans. They have a lot of manipulative traits to trigger people. Whatever they say is hardly recognizable, it confuses a person to this extent that makes a person feel that they are crazy. They alter the truth in such a way, and they think lying would serve them in the end.

DARK PSYCHOLOGY AND MANIPULATION

They Play the Victim Role

People having a Dark Side or dark psychology are good at manipulating. They tend to play victim even if they are guilty in the situation would make the other person feel that everything that happens was their fault where they are not responsible.

For manipulating and making situations in such a way that they turn into a victim. They would go to any extent to attest that they have nothing to do with the situation. They are really in that zone no matter what happens.

They are so good with the alteration of words that nobody even questions them in the situation. They are Masters when it comes to playing the victim role. They will play The Victim's role to clear the situation. They will play The Victim card to get out of the situation. They won't care about how and what it costs to people out on the other side. They don't want to be jammed in a place that can be harmful to them. No matter if they are turning parasites on others. They only look for the good in themselves and no one else. They only want betterment in every situation and don't spare anyone when it comes to this.

They Are Not Sincere

People having a Dark Side of the mind are really good manipulators. They are not sincere to anybody because they can put anyone down.

Anybody who comes into their space is a threat to them. They love watching others going down, and they are willing to do anything bad.

They would lie almost anywhere, and they would give the appearance of weakness because if it suits current needs, they will do whatever it would take. They would elaborate on situations in such a way that it would look so effective.

People having Dark Psychology perceive that it can harm anybody and their surroundings. Their life is so tamed that they are not loyal to anybody. They are not sincere. Sincerity is the best thing a person can hold. They are not only lying to themselves, but they are also lying to every other person around them. They are not a truthful friend to be with. They are not faithful. They would do anything to make them dominating and greater no matter if the person they are harming is their blood relation. They don't see relationships are close enough. No matter what outcome it would bring later on.

It Often Looks Like the Are Hypocrite

They are not truthful to anybody and themselves. They keep on lying about situations. They are playing with other people's minds that they sometimes forget what they are doing and what reaction would lead to the end. They often show people what they are called like they are not their real selves. Being genuine is about being true to yourself and the people surrounding you in every situation of life, which is why life has a set of events, and it seems to be the most trivial of occurrences. To approach life successfully, it is necessary to make the decisions that will divide the best that are the best outcome and at any given moment. A person has to be truthful and from to the best of their personalities and their need to be authentic. Every person is fake while going on the best things about our scenarios and they think that it is necessary to be true to themselves. They know that they don't settle for less. They try to be a wannabe in these situations. They put on a mask on a face to hide the real personality because the dark triad of a mind that is overlapping is a genuine and truthful personality.

They Can Get Extremely Aggressive

They have difficulty controlling their emotions no matter how much they try. They always come up with the reaction to situations and anything that is caused because of their darker side damages their professional reputation. It is also a threat to their productivity, and eventually, they end up losing everything. In normal circumstances, it is very easy to maintain calm and composed, but sometimes when things get out of hand, and other impulsive reactions trigger people to get aggressive because they can't control the words in the actions and whatever they are doing. They feel that they have complete freedom of how they want to react to certain situations, but that is not the truth. The reaction should come up with responsibilities. They should know that no matter what they are doing, they should never cross the limits, but sometimes, because of their aggressive behavior towards people and things, they forget their boundaries.

That's why many people fear the darker side. They don't want to expose it to others. They can be so sweet that it leaves a person in trauma to understand what they want because they are following a person and their insecurities and this also makes some very differences because they often lose the people they love. They can be very selfish and vicious whenever someone frames themselves from personal attacks and criticism, and there are dozens of pursuing ways of thinking that they can get whatever they want. They bully and threaten other people, and they won't let it stop until they destroy other people's mental peace.

HOW TO HANDLE MANIPULATORS IN YOUR LIFE IN 7 STEPS

A t one time or another, we've all been guilty of resorting to manipulation to get what we wanted. It is almost painful, now and then, never to talk without any kind of plan. We might resort to slight manipulation or persuasion whenever we need a friend's favor in trying to get them to go along with what we need them to do. When we need a co-worker to go along with our plan, we might need to turn to manipulation or threats to get them to take action. Leaders, managers and supervisors rely on some sort of manipulation techniques to either inspire (persuasion) or play on your emotions and anxieties to get you to listen and follow their instructions. Despite the negative connection to this word, deception is all around us.

Either you are being controlled, or you are manipulating.

Because we know by now, the manipulators will always want to be in control, to make themselves feel better to you and everyone else around them. To be the one pulling all the strings and encouraging everyone else to groove to their drumbeat. They will do whatever they can to try and rattle the confidence to do this, making you doubt yourself in second place. You may have done something like this before, even though you don't see yourself as a manipulator. Have you ever met a new laughing and joking friend at work when they tried to get us to know how to take a step back and tone it down? You may have felt a little insecure that everyone started warming up to the new colleague so easily, and you didn't like to believe your reputation could be challenged. That colleague may have been taken aback by this sudden remark, and what you would have done is to put a little seed of doubt in their minds that their behavior might not have been as acceptable as they thought. And maybe there was a buddy you were in danger of losing the promotion to, so you secretly point out all the "errors" they made to throw them off their game while playing on their insecurities. You may have also done this to you, when someone made a comment that caught you off guard, made you feel foolish and doubted your abilities.

Manipulators like to feel like those around them are never good enough. What's worse is that most of us still feel bad, to begin with, and we're worried that other people may find it too. This feeling has become so common now, with surveys showing that 70 percent of the population is experiencing this feeling of getting the name-imposter syndrome. Many who suffer from this syndrome are often feeling incompetent or feeling like a loser, according to the California Institute of Technology. Many dealing with Imposter Syndrome have a propensity to feel self-doubt and think they are intellectual fraud, no matter how much proof there is to indicate their success. Some studies showed that people who encountered this condition daily were mostly poorly performing (though they could do better) and were generally much more anxious than someone who treated Imposter Syndrome less often. After what they viewed as a disappointment, sufferers of imposter syndrome have suffered a higher, more severe loss of self-esteem. This experience also affects them harder than anyone else, and some studies have shown a clear link between Impostor Syndrome and feelings of guilt, embarrassment and self-sabotage.

Individuals with the Imposter Syndrome are exactly the type of individuals that manipulators want to pursue most. You are easy targets for them to prey on because they can tap into this psychological insecurity, and they can make your insecurities worse by constantly challenging your actions in such a way that you doubt your self-worth. They purposely do so to make you as distracted and off-balanced as possible, making it easier for them to strike when the time is right and take what they want from you.

HANDLING LIFETIME MANIPULATORS

Narcissists, sexual abusers and Discreet-aggressive manipulators. They're everywhere, and if you're sick of being a victim in their mind games, it's time to put an end to their control over you once and for all. No one has the right to exploit your insecurities and take advantage of them, whether their parents, brothers, uncles, aunts, associates, coworkers, superiors, supervisors, or clients. No one has the right to make you feel bad about yourself, and they're not going to push you to do anything you don't like. A relationship with a manipulator will last for years, especially if it is within your own family. It's more convenient to break ties with the manipulators you're not related to, but what do you do if they are your parents or siblings? Perhaps, people, you've grown up with and spent your entire life with?

YOUR HUMAN FREEDOMS

Those are the basic rights belonging to all of us, and no one has the right to violate your freedom with disrespect. When faced with manipulators, recalling those rights will help you steel your determination to fend off their attacks. Remember that you are responsible for your own life and happiness, and you should never put these two things in the hands of anyone else, particularly if that person happens to be a manipulator.

The next steps you need to handle the manipulators in your life are:

Staying Away from Them

This is the only way to get rid of their influence over you. If they aren't members of your immediate family, consider keeping away from them entirely, or breaking ties with them if you can because if they don't change their ways, it's doubtful the relationship will ever give you any food. Unless the manipulators are family members, you may not be able to fully break ties with them, but you may reduce the interaction time you are having with them. Stop spending time alone with them, stay "too busy" to have a conversation for too long, and be careful how much time you allow yourself to spend on them. Don't forget the basic rights that you hold.

Start protecting yourself against the intimidation of certain manipulators if they know their goals are lower. Manipulators whose personalities fall within the Dark Triad can also enjoy trying to mentally and emotionally threaten their victims, loving the power they feel when they know that they have struck fear in the hearts of others. Defend yourself from their abuse by recognizing that the manipulator clings to the vulnerabilities they consider to be yours. When you give in to what they want and play their game, you strengthen their idea that they are right. If you want to stand up for yourself and challenge them; instead, they tend to retreat like most manipulators behind all the bravado appear to be cowardly. You should never put yourself in a place where anyone will be able to see their true colors.

Do Not Let Them Push You

Even though you feel forced to make a decision, do not let them know. Be calm, stand firm and say clearly, "I'm going to need some time to think about it." If you start feeling the pressure on you, take a deep breath, and note that nobody has the right to push you to do something you don't want to do. You have the right to say no if you want to, and you don't need to feel bad about it. People's pleasures sometimes struggle with this move, since they have a strong desire to avoid disturbing others, even though they know that they are being manipulated. But you must stand your ground and let the manipulator know once and for all that they can't push and force you around like your feelings don't count for anything.

Know How to Say No

It's not the world's most relaxed feeling to say no, but your health and your needs will come first when you feel guilty. You owe the manipulator nothing, and they have no right to ask you to bend to their will (though that is exactly what they intend). You're not intentionally irritating anyone when you decide to say no, you respect yourself and you set your limits. Learning how to say no is how to stand up for yourself, realizing you are not going to be bullied around and saying no is within your rights if it no longer suits your happiness.

To Point Out the Repercussions

When you see that the manipulator places you in a position that you feel physically and emotionally violated, let the manipulator realize you are conscious of that by pointing out the potential implications of what they are attempting to do. Putting yourself one step ahead of them and letting them know you're completely safe from the repercussions will catch them and surprise and show you're not someone to be mixed up with. This will push them to re-evaluate their tactics and think twice before trying to take advantage of you in the future because they know you are not so easily fooled.

Don't Expect Much from Them

Particularly when you expect them to see things from your point of view. That does not happen because most manipulators tend to be self-absorbed individuals, concerned only with their needs and interests. We know less about the thoughts or views of other people, and they do not go out of their way to try to see it from your viewpoint. They don't have empathy and can't see their motivations past, so if you expect them to change their mind, you're only setting up for disappointment. Always expect them to change their ways, convince them to change their ways, or even attempt to fix them because 99.9 percent of the time isn't going to happen. Only because they want to change their ways, a manipulator will modify them, not because someone else told them to.

Accept Your Abilities

Coping with a manipulator needs a degree of emotional intelligence to be able to effectively fend them off. Patience, more patience, discipline, self-control, self-regulation and the resources you need to prevent you from losing your temper or responding in a way you may regret (some people can push your buttons far enough and enjoy seeing you fly off your handle). Getting a sense of your abilities and what you can do will help you stand your ground and keep things from going out of control.

Determine Your Boundaries

The next best thing you can do is to reframe the boundary phases for the partnerships that you can't remove. As challenging as accepting that your loved one can do such a thing, you need to come to terms with it so that you can then begin to focus on changing your expectations and setting the boundaries that you need to start protecting yourself. Take incremental steps to slowly establish certain limits, enabling them to occur progressively over time while building trust in the process. If they were somebody you've been to before for advice, start phasing it out by turning it over to someone else for advice. If they were someone you've earlier been looking for feedback, avoid actively searching it out, or ask for their opinion. They may still have it because they're so used to doing it, and when they do, just say thank you and leave it at that. You don't need to take their advice anymore; let it be a case of going in one ear and out the other. When you want to prevent a fight or have to contend with the manipulator wondering why you are setting limits against them, set the limits in smaller steps by doing so.

CONCLUSION

There is so much to learn about the psychological nature of people to prey on others. The truth is that all of humanity has the potential to victimize others. Yes, some try to sublimate this tendency while others choose to act upon their impulses. However, the most important thing for you is to understand your thoughts, perceptions and feelings that lead to predatory behavior so that you can learn to control yourself and use it for good.

One thing that is important to note is that manipulation often happens in families with parents who have narcissistic tendencies. In the case where there is parental alienation, a parent may use their child as a psychological weapon to abuse the other parent. The truth is that mind control, a form of dark psychology, happens in a system where people are—such as churches, families and workplaces.

Within each one of us lies this potential! You and I have the potential to harm others without cause, purpose, or explanation. This potential is considered complex—one that is even hard to define.

One thing you must note is that your shadow self is always standing right behind you—just outside your view. When you stand in direct light, you cast a shadow, right. The shadow is the part of yourself that you can't really see. Think about it for a moment, what lengths do you go to just to protect your self-image from unfamiliarity and flattery?

The truth is when you see another person's shadow, you realize that one can show gifts in one area of life and remain unaware of their evil behaviors in certain areas. Everyone is susceptible to this. Over the years, I have learned that working with my shadow has not only been a challenging but rewarding process, too. It is by looking at your darker side that you gain greater creativity, authenticity, personal awakening and energy. It is this subjective process that contributes to your maturity.

Realize that you cannot eliminate your darker side. Instead, it stays with you as your darker brother or sister. When we fail to see our darker self, that is when trouble ensues.

While our shadow self can operate on its own without our awareness—more like it is on autopilot—it causes us to do things we would not do voluntarily, and that is the reason behind regret. You find yourself saying things you wouldn't normally say. Your body language expresses emotions you would consciously not feel. In short, when you ignore your dark side, you end up hurting your relationships—with friends, spouse, or family, among others.

When you see others and yourself exactly as you are, you view the world around you with a clearer lens. Integrating your shadow self into everyday activities helps you approach your true self, hence offering you a realistic evaluation of who you are. In other words, you will not perceive yourself as being too small; neither will you feel as though you have a higher moral ground than others.

The reward of doing this plays a significant role in healing splits in your mind. It also helps unlock untapped potential and a world of new possibilities for your growth and development.

So, what are you still waiting for? It is time to embrace your dark side so that you allow the light inside you to radiate without fear of hurting others by being all that you are meant to be. Your dark side will help you overcome manipulation so that you can shine brighter!

Good Luck!

BONUS CHAPTER: 10
METHODS TO FOLLOW TO STOP BEING MANIPULATED AND BECOME INDEPENDENT AGAIN

At this point in your reading, I assume you have a clear understanding of manipulation with regards to what it is, how it happens and the techniques that are involved. Maybe you are reading this book because you have been manipulated or feel like you are being manipulated. Whatever the reason, we have come to the most important part: learning to defend ourselves from manipulators. When people realize they have been manipulated, they may feel ashamed, weak, used, or stupid. Generally, being manipulated sucks, especially after realizing that we have been unconsciously used to help other people to further their selfish agendas.

Chronic manipulation can have devastating effects on the victims. The most obvious effect is that the affected person develops a negative image of themselves and the world. This is true, especially for people who have been manipulated and had their bodies or minds abused. Some people stop trusting everyone and everything out of fear of being manipulated again. Nobody wants to have their worldviews negatively affected by intruders.

All the same, there is some good news. The good news is that just like we can put measures in place to prevent us from falling ill, we can also implement some to prevent and discourage manipulation. Manipulation will only affect us if we allow it or if we fail to recognize it before and while it happens. By identifying manipulation before it occurs, we can retain control over our lives. Even if we are already being manipulated by applying these effective anti-manipulation tactics, we can overcome the vice and reclaim our beautiful lives.

We are going to talk about powerful ways to avoid or reverse manipulation. Some of the ideas we shall highlight might not be desirable or effective in every situation. That said and done, let us go straight to the first method of avoiding manipulation.

#1 METHOD
UNDERSTAND YOUR RIGHTS

The main reason that you will feel as if someone is manipulating you is that you will feel as if your rights have been violated. However, you might fail to even re-alize that someone is manipulating you if you have no idea what fundamental rights you are entitled to. As long as you stick to your lane and do not harm other people or interfere with their lives, you remain on the safe side. Fundamental rights are the acceptable boundaries that define the extent to which one person can affect the life of another. Therefore, one of the most effective ways that can help you to keep manipu-lators away is to understand where your rights start and end. Below are some of the common fundamental human rights:

- Everyone has the right to be accorded respect. If you re-alize that someone is disrespecting you, it might be a sign of manipulation.

- Everyone has the right to determine their priorities. If you decide to prioritize yourself, nobody should try to in-terfere with that.

- Everyone has the free will to express their wants, opin-ions and feelings. As we have already seen, manipulation happens by taking away free will.

- Everyone has the right to refuse something without being made to feel guilty. This is very important because if you realize that you do not want something, saying "no" should be respected.

- Everyone has the right to have opinions that differ from those of others. Disagreements are normal. Therefore, nobody should mistreat you in any way for holding different opinions.

- Everyone has the right to create and live their own healthy and happy life. In short, if anything threatens to take this right away, such as a toxic friendship, you have the right to cut it down.

Finally, and very important to our topic of avoiding manipulation, everyone has the right to protect themselves from being emotionally, physically, or mentally threatened. If you feel this right is being violated, feel free to object and move away.

#2 METHOD
MAINTAIN YOUR DISTANCE

It is easy to detect a manipulator because they tend to show their true colors when faced with different situations or when interacting with different people. As humans, we are allowed to adapt to situations and people. However, with toxic people, their variations are extreme. A manipulator can be highly polite when with you, but when they meet someone, they have less regard for, they transform into overly rude or aggressive with them. Similarly, they might seem helpless at one moment but become very controlling in the next. This is a sure red flag that the person is unstable and unreliable and that it will only be a matter of time before they extend the same to you.

The best reaction when you come across such a person is to maintain your healthy distance. A healthy distance means you might not necessarily cut them off completely, but you do not put yourself in situations that might make it easy for them to control you. You should avoid engaging with such a person as much as you can, and only doing it when you need to. We have seen that chronic manipulators do it out of psychological complications, and it might be easier to avoid them than try to change them. However, this is a personal choice since the person might be an acquaintance who might feel the need to assist them out of their bad habit.

#3 METHOD
UNDERSTAND THEM

It is very important to understand that manipulation can be a manifestation of a psychological problem. If you understand something, then you can determine how to deal with it. For example, we do not scold babies for soiling their clothes or keeping us awake all night because we know it is beyond their control. As they grow up, these habits improve. In the same way, you should look at a manipulator as someone who is experiencing a problem with themselves. Manipulative people tend to possess low self-esteem, lower willpower, uncertain reasons to live and an irresistible urge for chaos and drama.

That said, you should not take whatever they do or say offensively. Their way of expression is affected such that it does not go well with normal people. One of the reasons they might tend to control others is that they feel inferior and need to hurt others so they can feel better. Others do not even realize that their actions affect others because they lack empathy. In short, if we understand that manipulation is a form of the disease, then we can take any manipulative approaches lightly. In this way, the manipulator does not gain any power or control over us.

#4 METHOD
HIDE YOUR WEAKNESSES

One way to enable it to happen is by allowing outsiders to know our weaknesses. A manipulator's agenda is usually to find out the weaknesses of their victims and then using them to evoke the feeling of inadequacy, guilt, shame, blame, or weakness. Therefore, not unless it is very necessary, or the person you are opening up to has proven to be real and trustworthy, always keep your weaknesses hidden. The downside to opening up even to real friends is that you never know when the friendship might end.

To some extent, sharing our weaknesses is not even necessary. Weaknesses are part of being human, and everyone has a share of the same. Therefore, if you can keep your shortfalls to yourself and feel satisfied with them, it can be the best defense against manipulation. After all, everyone has their flaws, and they do not go around preaching about them. Once the manipulator has no shortcuts to accessing our most powerful emotions, they cannot succeed in invading our lives. In short, know what to share with others and what to keep to yourself.

#5 METHOD
DO NOT ASK FOR PERMISSION

In our upbringing, we are taught to always ask for things to be done for us. We had to ask for food rather than prepare it ourselves. We also had to require permission before going out or sleeping over at a friends' house. Requesting permission was meant to keep us in good standing with everyone by avoiding doing what would otherwise offend them. Unfortunately, this training led to conditioning whereby to do something; we need to seek permission or validation even as adults. Manipulators have taken advantage of this kind gesture and turned it into their artillery. They want us to feel tied to imaginary ideals and rules that we must consult with some authority before taking action. Worse still, they install themselves as these authorities, which we must consult.

Honestly, asking for permission, especially to do things in one's personal life is outdated. It is about time we stopped being concerned with the opinions of others about our life decisions. Otherwise, if we need others to approve or disapprove of all our decisions, we get cast into an abyss of confinement.

For example, parents should not decide who their children should marry. While this used to be a common practice in the past, things have changed. Arranged marriages risk pitting two people who have no connection together. Such relationships feel like prisons for both partners, and usually, they end in disaster. Therefore, to avoid manipulation of this kind, we should make our decisions without seeking the opinions of others (manipulators).

#6 METHOD
IGNORE MANIPULATORS

If you cannot move away from a person that you already know is manipulative, apply the shield of ignorance. One of the mistakes that we make when dealing with such people is giving them the attention they so desire. Once they get the attention, they gain the upper hand in initiating the mind poisoning process. Therefore, if you see or suspect that a manipulative person is making moves on you, just ignore them. For instance, if someone is giving you too many compliments yet you are not acquainted with them, resort to ignoring them. You can tell them that the compliments are enough and ignore them henceforth.

One risk of ignoring manipulative people is that it might trigger more aggressiveness in them. They are usually fighting with their inner selves and will pour out the anger if they feel they are being ignored. This does not mean that you should not apply ignorance where necessary. On the brighter side, you can ignore them, hoping their human side is still alive. When a normal person feels ignored, they pull back and stop their advances. Therefore, assume that this is the response that they will give. If they resort to aggression, you can take appropriate action such as reporting them. We will go into this point later.

#7 METHOD
JUDGE YOUR JUDGE

You are the only person in this universe who knows yourself in the best way. Even if scientists studied you for a decade, they would never understand you as much as you understand yourself. Do you agree? Well, if you said yes, then learn to trust yourself and stop the narrative of doubting your decisions or instincts. You have learned that a manipulator tries to sow doubt in you through techniques such as crazymaking, twisting reality, lying and gaslighting. If you study these methods well, you will realize they are all pegged on self-doubt. In short, if you trust other people more than you do yourself, it is a recipe for manipulation.

The best way to start trusting in yourself is by taking away the power of others to define you. In the world, everyone you meet has a different opinion from you. Imagine what would happen if you believed everything that everyone you met said about you. You would not only be confused but also hurt. Therefore, focus on your understanding of yourself and ignore what other people think or say about you. Once you have strong beliefs about yourself, it makes it hard for manipulative people to interfere with you. Your beliefs act as the shield against toxic invasion.

#8 METHOD
RECORD INTERACTIONS TOXIC PEOPLE

You might have probably started seeing this as a method that is a little overboard, but trust me; it might save you psychological torture. Remember we said that manipulative people have the habit of saying things and later denying them. They might also say or do bad things to you and later turn the tables, so you end up being the bad guy. To overcome such incidences, you can record the interactions with the people you have identified as manipulative. Think about it; if you provided evidence that someone said something while they are at the helm of denying it, you not only shame them but also discourage them from repeating it.

In today's world of smartphones and computers, recording a chat or phone conversation is as easy as pressing a button. You can keep the conversations you have with suspicious people. During something like a call, when the manipulation starts, you can start recording. Even in face-to-face conversations, if someone is trying to blackmail you, you can secretly tape the conversation using your phone or discreet devices. If it ever gets to a point where they start denying saying or doing something, provide the evidence. This is enough to silence them permanently.

#9 METHOD
ALWAYS GRAB NEW OPPORTUNITIES

Today's society wants people to stay stuck in the same play and store all their eggs in one basket. People around us are busy telling us what to do and what they expect of us. To them, being employed, taking a mortgage, getting married at 25 and doing the same thing everyone is doing is the right thing. To them, being ambitious is deviating from the right way of life, and they start seeing you as an outcast. This is a complex form of manipulation in that they want to indirectly influence your life and make it as predictable as possible. A predictable life is easy to invade and control.

Ambitious people are, at times, seen as greedy, selfish, proud and arrogant. It is not uncommon to have these names branded on hardworking people. The trick to avoiding this type of mind control is to keep grabbing new opportunities and remaining unpredictable. Chasing new experiences, building new relationships, starting new businesses and applying for better jobs keep a person independent and in control of their lives. When someone is unpredictable and in full control of themselves, manipulative people cannot bring them down. Therefore, grab any new opportunities which present themselves and ignore what others say.

#10 METHOD
CALL THEM OUT

It is possible that a manipulator might have controlled people for a long time because nobody has ever confronted them. This is an assumption, but it does not make the method any less effective. Manipulators can be bullies too, and bullies are weak people who torture others who feel helpless before them. In short, do not let the manipulator feel like you know they are using you but fear speaking it up. Allowing them to continue uninterrupted will only increase their power over you as well as the severity of their behavior. When it becomes clear that someone is trying to mess with your mind, let them know that you are uncomfortable with it.

Calling out on the manipulator's behavior might have several positive effects. First, they will realize that you are awake enough to realize that they are attempting mind tricks on you. Toxic people hate and are scared of people with strong consciousness and self-esteem. Second, by calling them out, you might be the first person who has ever stood up to them. The shock of being discovered plus the shame that comes with it can be a strong enough deterrent. If this is the case, it might force them to realize the extent of their behavior. Assuming they are not chronic manipulators, they can change their ways.

REFERENCES

14 Signs of Psychological and Emotional Manipulation. (n.d.). Retrieved from https://www.psychologyto-day.com/us/blog/communication-success/201510/14-signs-psychological-and-emotional-manipulation

3 Signs of an Inconspicuous Predator in Your Midst. (n.d.). Retrieved from https://www.psychologyto-day.com/us/blog/shadow-boxing/201406/3-signs-inconspicu-ous-predator-in-your-midst

4 Signs of A Machiavellian Personality Disorder. (2018, August 27). Retrieved from https://www.spring.org.uk/2018/08/machiavellian-per-sonality-disorder.php

Abrams, B. S. L. (2018, September 29). Are you being emotionally manipulated? Retrieved from https://www.eb-ony.com/love-relationships/are-you-being-emotionally-manip-ulated/

Barnes, S., & Barnes, S. (n.d.). 9 signs you're being emo-tionally manipulated by your significant other. Retrieved from https://hellogiggles.com/love-sex/9-signs-youre-emotion-ally-manipulated-significant-other/

Boissoneault, L. (2017, May 22). The true story of brain-washing and how it shaped America. Retrieved from https://www.smithsonianmag.com/history/true-story-brainwashing-and-how-it-shaped-america-180963400/

Brainwashing. (n.d.). Retrieved from https://www.mer-riam-webster.com/dictionary/brainwashing

Brainwashing. (2019, September 14). Retrieved from https://en.wikipedia.org/wiki/Brainwashing

Britannica, T. E. of E. (n.d.). Brainwashing. Retrieved from https://www.britannica.com/topic/brainwashing

Brown, J. (2018, July 12). This is how normal life feels as a psychopath. Retrieved from https://me-dium.com/s/story/this-is-how-normal-life-feels-as-a-psycho-path-2294c3f36311

Brown, L. (2019, August 24). 10 disturbing signs of emotional manipulation that most people miss. Retrieved from https://ideapod.com/signs-emotional-manipulation/

Byrne, T. (2015, October 15). Beware of the emotional predator. Retrieved from https://goodmenproject.com/fea-tured-content/beware-of-the-emotional-predator-dg/

Cherry, K. (2019, July 15). 5 myths about hypnosis de-bunked. Retrieved from https://www.verywellmind.com/what-is-hypnosis-2795921

Clarke, J. (2019, April 12). How to recognize someone with covert narcissism. Retrieved from https://www.verywellmind.com/understanding-the-cov-ert-narcissist-4584587

Cohut, M. (2017, September 1). Hypnosis: What is it, and does it work? Retrieved from https://www.medicalnew-stoday.com/articles/319251.php

Comparison of light triad to dark triad. (n.d.). [Online image]. Retrieved from https://www.frontiersin.org/files/Arti-cles/438704/fpsyg-10-00467-HTML/image_m/fpsyg-10-00467-t006.jpg

Covert Conversational Hypnosis Webinar. (n.d.). Re-trieved from https://www.transformdestiny.com/hypno-sis/covert-conversational-hypnosis-home-study.asp

Covert Hypnosis. (n.d.). Retrieved from https://www.the-secret-of-mindpower-and-nlp.com/Cov-ert-hypnosis.html

Dilts, R. B. (1999). What is NLP? Retrieved September 30, 2019, from http://www.nlpu.com/NLPU_WhatIsNLP.html

Effect of emotional intelligence on job performance. (n.d.). [Online image] Retrieved from https://www.re-searchgate.net/profile/Daniel_Newman9/publica-tion/41087511/fig-ure/fig3/AS:668543704125448@1536404648453/Cascading-model-of-emotional-intelligence-El-The-cascading-model-is-based-on-the.png

Emotional Intelligence (EQ): The Premier Provider - Tests, Training, Certification, and Coaching. (n.d.). Retrieved from https://www.talentsmart.com/articles/9-Signs-Youre-Dealing-With-an-Emotional-Manipulator-2147446691-p-1.html

Emotional Predators. (n.d.). Retrieved from https://psy-chopathyawareness.wordpress.com/tag/emotional-predators/

Experts Say These 7 Common Phrases Are Actually Emotional Manipulation. (n.d.). Retrieved from https://www.bustle.com/p/what-does-emotional-manipu-lation-look-like-7-lines-people-may-use-to-control-others-to-be-aware-of-18175851

Get the Life You Want Starting NOW! (2010, April 4). Retrieved from https://www.nlppower.com/

Holland, K. (2018, February 13). How to recognize the signs of emotional manipulation and what to do. Retrieved September 30, 2019, from https://www.health-line.com/health/mental-health/emotional-manipulation

How To Recognize The 8 Signs Of Emotional Manipula-tion. (2019, August 5). Retrieved from https://livebol-dandbloom.com/02/relationships/emotional-manipulation

How to Spot Common Predator Characteristics. (2018, January 22). Retrieved from https://www.sterlingvolun-teers.com/blog/2018/01/spot-common-predator-characteris-tics/

Hypnosis. (n.d.). Retrieved October 1, 2019, from https://www.apa.org/topics/hypnosis/

Hypnosis. (n.d.). Retrieved from https://www.psychologytoday.com/us/basics/hypnosis

Hypnosis. (2019, September 20). Retrieved from https://en.wikipedia.org/wiki/Hypnosis.

Hypnotherapy - Hypnosis. (n.d.). Retrieved from https://www.webmd.com/mental-health/mental-health-hypnotherapy#1

Kandola, A. (n.d.). Neuro-linguistic programming (NLP): Does it work? Retrieved from https://www.medicalnewstoday.com/articles/320368.php

Kassel, G. (n.d.). 11 signs you're dating a narcissist — And how to get out. Retrieved September 30, 2019, from https://www.healthline.com/health/mental-health/am-i-dating-a-narcissist#15

Khazan, O. (2014, March 1). The dark psychology of being a good comedian. Retrieved from https://www.theatlantic.com/health/archive/2014/02/the-dark-psychology-of-being-a-good-comedian/284104/

La Fayette, Marie-Madeleine Pioche de La Vergne de. (1780). La Princesse de Cleves. Paris.

Layton, J. (2019, May 1). How brainwashing works. Retrieved from https://science.howstuffworks.com/life/inside-the-mind/human-brain/brainwashing.htm

Leary, M. R. (2015, December). Emotional responses to interpersonal rejection. Retrieved from https://www.ncbi.nlm.nih.gov/pmc/articles/PMC4734881/

Machiavelli, Niccolò. (2004). The Prince. London: Penguin.

Machiavellianism. (2019, September 24). Retrieved from https://en.wikipedia.org/wiki/Machiavellianism

McLarty, B.D. (2015). [Online image]. The devil at work: Understanding the dark side of personality and its impact on performance. Retrieved from https://www.seman-ticscholar.org/paper/The-Devil-at-Work%3A-Understanding-the-Dark-Side-of-McLarty/52d642007166340842ec2c3ba15e91672e941fb6

Meet the Machiavellians. (n.d.). Retrieved from https://www.psychologytoday.com/us/blog/machiavelli-ans-gulling-the-rubes/201509/meet-the-machiavellians

Melley, T. (2011). Brain warfare: The covert sphere, ter-rorism, and the legacy of the cold War. Grey Room, (45), 19–40. Retrieved from https://www.jstor.org/stable/41342501?read-now=1&seq=1#page_scan_tab_contents

Model of hypnosis. (n.d.). [Online image]. Retrieved from https://tedmoreno.com/2014/09/10/hypnosis-101-what-is-hypnosis/

Moore, R. (2018, September 19). The brainwashing myth. Retrieved from http://theconversation.com/the-brainwashing-myth-99272

Morris, G., & Morris, G. (n.d.). Behavioral indicators of antisocial personality disorder. Retrieved from https://www.ac-tivebeat.com/your-health/6-behavioral-indicators-of-antiso-cial-personality-disorder/?utm_me-dium=cpc&utm_source=google&utm_cam-paign=AB_GGL_US_MOBl-SearchMarketing_TR&utm_con-tent=s_c_303621126873&cus_widget=&utm_term=psychologi-cal&cus_teaser=kwd-10865291&utm_acid=3040947159&utm_caid=1599827680&utm_agid=63349425987&utm_os=&gclid=EAlalQob-ChMlhLfKyKrn5AlVA4TlChOvbgW_EAAYAiAAEglIXfD_BwE

Narcissism. (n.d.). Retrieved from https://www.psychol-ogytoday.com/us/basics/narcissism

Narcissism. (2019, September 27). Retrieved from https://en.wikipedia.org/wiki/Narcissism

Narcissistic Personality Disorder. (n.d.). Retrieved from https://www.psychologytoday.com/us/conditions/narcis-sistic-personality-disorder

Narcissistic Personality Disorder. (2017, November 18). Retrieved from https://www.mayoclinic.org/diseases-condi-tions/narcissistic-personality-disorder/symptoms-causes/syc-20366662

Narcissistic Personality Disorder. (2019, July 12). Re-trieved from https://www.helpguide.org/articles/mental-disor-ders/narcissistic-personality-disorder.htm

Nedelman, M. (2018, February 13). Are you susceptible to brainwashing? Retrieved from https://www.cnn.com/2018/02/13/health/brainwashing-mind-control-patty-hearst/index.html.

Neuro-Linguistic Programming (NLP). (n.d.) Retrieved from https://www.skillsyouneed.com/ps/nlp.html

Neuro-Linguistic Programming Therapy. (n.d.). Re-trieved from https://www.psychologytoday.com/us/therapy-types/neuro-linguistic-programming-therapy

NLP model of therapeutic change. [Online image]. (n.d.). Retrieved from https://i.pinimg.com/origi-nals/20/67/07/206707645d0afe5d59610322d25b920a.jpg

NLP Training Courses & Neuro-Linguistic Programming Techniques. (n.d.). Retrieved from http://www.thenlpcom-pany.com/

Nuccitelli, M. (2006). Dark psychology - Dark side of human consciousness concept. Retrieved from https://www.ipredator.co/dark-psychology/

Nuccitelli, M. (2006). Dark psychology - Dark side of human consciousness definition. (n.d.). Retrieved from https://www.darkpsychology.co/dark-psychology/

Nuccitelli, M. (2019). Dark psychology - Definition of the psychological construct. Retrieved from https://www.darkpsychology.co/dark-psychology-definition/

Panger, G. T. (2017). Emotion in Social Media [Dissertation].

Platform. (n.d.). Retrieved from https://www.alegion.com/solution/platform?utm_source=adwords&utm_medium=ppc&utm_term=nlp neuro linguistic&utm_campaign=NLP&hsa_net=adwords&hsa_ver=3&hsa_ad=356028543502&hsa_src=s&hsa_cam=2038305254&hsa_acc=1622984630&hsa_kw=nlp neuro linguistic&hsa_tgt=kwd-310275137465&hsa_grp=70406593365&hsa_mt=p&gclid=EAIaIQobChMIycjyvp_s5AIVsCCtBh2JAA_NEAAYAyAAEgl8zPD_BwE

Plinkleton. (2015, October 10). Study finds some psychopaths have enhanced recognition of others' emotions. Retrieved from https://www.psypost.org/2015/08/study-finds-some-psychopaths-have-enhanced-recognition-of-others-emotions-37116

Predation. (2019, September 29). Retrieved from https://en.wikipedia.org/wiki/Predation

Psychological Manipulation. (2019, September 20). Retrieved from https://en.wikipedia.org/wiki/Psychological_manipulation

Psychopathy. (n.d.). Retrieved from https://www.sciencedirect.com/topics/medicine-and-dentistry/psychopathy

Psychopathy. (n.d.). Retrieved from https://www.psychologytoday.com/us/basics/psychopathy

Psychopathy: A Misunderstood Personality Disorder. (n.d.). Retrieved from https://www.psychologi-calscience.org/news/releases/psychopathy-a-misunderstood-personality-disorder.html

R Blair, R. J. (2013, June). Psychopathy: cognitive and neural dysfunction. Retrieved from https://www.ncbi.nlm.nih.gov/pmc/articles/PMC3811089/

Ramey, S. (2017, January 23). How to escape the cage built by an emotional predator. Retrieved from https://ex-ploringyourmind.com/escape-cage-built-emotional-predator/

Recognize Emotional Predator Traits and Behaviors. (2019, July 23). Retrieved from https://emotionalpreda-tors.com/recognize-emotional-predator-traits-and-behaviors/

Resnick, B. (2017, March 7). The dark psychology of de-humanization, explained. Retrieved from https://www.vox.com/science-and-health/2017/3/7/14456154/dehumanization-psychology-ex-plained

Rossner, J. (2014). Looking for Mr. Goodbar. New York: Simon and Schuster Paperbacks.

Selfcarehaven. (2018, May 12). Dating emotional preda-tors: Signs to look out for. Retrieved from https://selfcare-haven.wordpress.com/2014/08/29/dating-emotional-preda-tors-signs-to-look-out-for/

Signs and Traits of Narcissists, Crazymakers, Emotional Manipulators, Unsafe People. (n.d.). Retrieved from http://thinklikeablackbelt.com/blog/signs-and-traits-of-emotional-predators/

Storytel AB. (n.d.). Dark psychology: Learn to influence anyone using mind control, manipulation and deception with se-cret techniques of dark persuasion, undetected mind control, mind games, hypnotism and brainwashing. Retrieved from https://www.storytel.com/se/sv/books/638795-Dark-

Psychology-Learn-To-Influence-Anyone-Using-Mind-Control-Manipulation-And-Deception-With-Secret-Techniques-Of-Dark-Persuasion-Undetected-Mind-Control-Mind-Games-Hypnotism-And-Brainwashing

Taylor, B. (2018, October 8). Machiavellianism, cognition, and emotion: Understanding how the Machiavellian thinks, feels, and thrives. Retrieved from https://psychcentral.com/lib/machiavellianism-cognition-and-emotion-understanding-how-the-machiavellian-thinks-feels-and-thrives/

Team, G. T. E. (2018, December 2). Neuro-linguistic programming (NLP). Retrieved from https://www.goodtherapy.org/learn-about-therapy/types/neuro-linguistic-programming

The 30 Most Disturbing Human Experiments in History. (n.d.). Retrieved from https://www.bestpsychologydegrees.com/30-most-disturbing-human-experiments-in-history/

The Art of Brainwashing. (n.d.). Retrieved from https://www.psychologytoday.com/us/blog/brain-chemistry/201803/the-art-brainwashing

The Human Predator—Spot and Deal With Them—Open Minds Foundation. (2018, April 5). Retrieved from https://www.openmindsfoundation.org/faces_of_undue_influence/what-is-manipulation/human-predator/

The Stealthiest Predator. (n.d.). Retrieved from https://www.psychologytoday.com/us/articles/201805/the-stealthiest-predator

Therapy, H. (2019, August 31). What is Machiavellianism in psychology? Retrieved from https://www.harley-therapy.co.uk/counselling/machiavellianism-psychology.htm

Watching out for Emotional Predators. Are You Being Brainwashed into Becoming a Manipulation or Emotional Abuse Victim? (2019, June 13). Retrieved from https://loveandabuse.com/watching-out-for-emotional-predators-are-you-be-ing-brainwashed-into-becoming-a-manipulation-or-emotional-abuse-victim/

What is Neuro-Linguistic Programming - NLP - and Why Learn It? (2019, September 14). Retrieved from https://inlpcenter.org/what-is-neuro-linguistic-program-ming-nlp/

What is NLP? (n.d.). Retrieved from http://www.nlp.com/what-is-nlp/

Made in United States
Orlando, FL
21 December 2021

12351324R00085